"Every page of *The Action Mindset Workbook for Teens* is jam-packed with facts, fun activities, and science-backed strategies to help tweens and teens acquire all the self-awareness, confidence, courage, and coping skills they need to challenge their own unhelpful thoughts, boost their motivation, deal with stress and anxiety, face their fears, and feel empowered to take action toward their goals. This book is a must-read for every middle and high school student on the planet!"

—**Phyllis L. Fagell, LCPC**, school counselor, therapist, journalist, and author of the books
Middle School Matters and *Middle School Superpowers*

"Most teens know what they want: A sense of autonomy, accomplishment, belonging, and validation from others. But to get there, it takes both courage and the skills and affirming attitudes required to overcome their fears and translate vision into action. What they, what YOU, will find in this book is the toolkit you need to master these skills and integrate these attitudes into a new sense of who you are."

—**Louis G. Castonguay, PhD**, liberal arts professor of psychology at Penn State University,
and former president of the Society for Psychotherapy Research

"The world can seem scary and overwhelming. Many teens cope by withdrawing or shutting down.
The Action Mindset Workbook for Teens has readers examine how shutting down impacts their lives, and walks them through action steps that boost their sense of power and resiliency. Chapters like How to Quiet Your Inner Voice of Doom provide teens with coping skills that will last a lifetime."

—**Kathryn Stamoulis, PhD, LMHC**, expert in adolescent development

"It's never been easy to transition from childhood to adulthood as you navigate complex friendships, build a sense of identity, manage difficult adults, and meet the demands of school. Thankfully Mary Alvord and Anne McGrath have created this fantastic workbook, which brings you the best-tested practices for dealing with life, in an easy-to-follow format. The skills you'll learn here will stay with you through high school, college, and beyond."

—**Seth Gillihan, PhD**, licensed psychologist, host of the *Think Act Be* podcast,
and author of *Mindful Cognitive Behavioral Therapy*

T0000588

"Therapy isn't an option for everyone, but *The Action Mindset Workbook for Teens* is. Chock-full of relatable examples, this handy resource helps teens learn, then practice, the skills they need to conquer long-standing counterproductive habits, replacing them with more effective ways of responding to self-consciousness, perfectionism, lethargy, and more. Teenage readers will emerge feeling energized and hopeful, with skills that will serve them well for a lifetime."

—**Dawn Huebner, PhD,** parent coach, author of *Outsmarting Worry*, and coauthor of *The A-Z Guide to Exposure* and *Outsmarting Worry*

"A superb offering from Mary Alvord and Anne McGrath! Drawing on Alvord's extensive clinical experience and firm grasp of classic and 'third-wave' cognitive behavioral therapy (CBT) principles, they have created a wonderful workbook. Skillfully written to communicate to teens troubled by anxiety, avoidance, or depression, it effectively introduces key concepts and practice exercises. It will facilitate individual or group psychotherapy, but may be explored alone or in classroom settings. Excellent!"

—**Kenneth E. Towbin, MD**, clinical professor in the department of psychiatry and behavioral sciences at The George Washington University School of Medicine

"Alvord and McGrath have given teens an incredible resource for managing difficult emotions. *The Action Mindset Workbook for Teens* uses approachable language, real-world examples, and practical guidance to help others live a healthier and more fulfilled life. This book is a road map for how to cut out avoidance and change your life through action, and I can't wait to introduce it to the teens in my life!"

—**Regine Galanti, PhD**, director of Long Island Behavioral Psychology, and author of *Anxiety Relief for Teens* and *When Harley Has Anxiety*

"*The Action Mindset Workbook for Teens* is a user-friendly, engaging resource in which every teen will find something helpful. Drawing on key evidence-based tools, young people can learn more about their doubts and fears, change common patterns that hold them back, and become better positioned to pursue what matters most to them. There has never been a more important time to offer young people tools they can really use that build resilience."

—**Mary Ann McCabe, PhD, ABPP**, associate clinical professor of pediatrics at The George Washington University School of Medicine, and advocate for youth mental health

SIMPLE CBT SKILLS TO HELP YOU CONQUER FEAR & SELF-DOUBT
& TAKE STEPS TOWARD WHAT REALLY MATTERS

THE
ACTION MINDSET
WORKBOOK
FOR TEENS

MARY KARAPETIAN ALVORD, PHD · ANNE MCGRATH, MA

Instant Help Books
An Imprint of New Harbinger Publications, Inc.

Publisher's Note

INSTANT HELP, the Clock Logo, and NEW HARBINGER are trademarks of New Harbinger Publications, Inc.

New Harbinger Publications is an employee-owned company.

Copyright © 2023 by Mary Karapetian Alvord and Anne McGrath

Instant Help Books
An imprint of New Harbinger Publications, Inc.
5674 Shattuck Avenue
Oakland, CA 94609
www.newharbinger.com

All Rights Reserved
Cover and book design by Amy Shoup
Illustrations by Sara Christian
Acquired by Tesilya Hanauer
Edited by Karen Schader

Library of Congress Cataloging-in-Publication Data on file

Printed in the United States of America

25   24   23

10   9   8   7   6   5   4   3   2   1   First Printing

To our grandchildren,
our own future teenagers

CONTENTS

FOREWORD

If you are a middle school or high school student experiencing insecurity about facing new challenges or social situations or taking other healthy risks, this workbook is for you. If anxiety, fear, and self-doubts have paralyzed you into inaction, this workbook offers ways to free yourself from feelings of being stuck. The book's activities will challenge you to move from avoidance behaviors that are self-defeating to proactive ones that are empowering. You will learn how to tolerate the discomfort that often prevents people from stepping outside their comfort zone. The ultimate goal is to help you build self-esteem and a sense of confidence so you can fully engage in and enjoy your life. Actually, many adults could benefit from going through these exercises!

Changing an avoidance habit, as is true of any behavior change, is going to be hard work. But the fact that you're reading this book is a good sign—an indication that you're motivated to try. Over the past forty years, my research and clinical work have centered on exploring how people change, and we have found that the process happens in steps or stages. Motivation is an important contributor to success, a key factor in making any changes in our lives.

How do people change? First, you need to become interested in the need for change and understand how it will benefit you. You next have to find the courage to accept the discomfort that will come with stepping into unfamiliar territory, and make a plan of action. Then you need to take that first step, and try on new behaviors to see how they fit. These actions will not be spectacularly successful overnight. As with riding a bike, you have to learn and practice new behaviors. Persistence pays off when we talk about finding better, more constructive ways to live.

There are many obstacles that can get in the way of making a change. We have identified several states of mind—five Rs—that commonly interfere with moving forward. Maybe you haven't found your motivation yet and are happy with the status quo, **reveling** in doing what you've been doing. Or perhaps you **rationalize** that change isn't really necessary, or that it won't do any good. If another person is urging that you change, you may feel **rebellious**. Sometimes you may simply be **reluctant** to leave your comfort zone, even when you know you need to do so. And sometimes people get discouraged and just give up, **resigned** to life as it is. These ways of resisting change keep us stuck in behavior patterns that do not make us happy or healthy.

Your challenge as you work your way through this book is to identify what behavior change is needed to make your life better, overcome your resistance, plan those first brave steps, and figure out how to take them. The activities will help you move away from self-defeating thinking and inaction by guiding you through the basic stages of changing the way you respond to challenges in your life.

This focus on learning how to change is one of this workbook's most helpful features. Like the old proverb says, it teaches a starving person to fish rather than giving them a fish. Developing an action mindset now will help you face and rise to many different challenges throughout your life. I find the illustrations of how teens in common situations might proceed toward action to be particularly useful. These models can help you test your thinking, consider your options, and come up with positive ways to behave that will contribute to your emotional growth and well-being.

In her years of practice as a psychologist, Mary Alvord has talked with, listened to, and worked with many middle and high school youth. This book's innovative and multidimensional approach, based on her deep understanding of the teenage experience, the principles of how change happens, and well-established strategies of cognitive behavioral therapy (CBT), can help all teens face the insecurities, sadness, and anxieties that are preventing them from embracing and enjoying life. The workbook does not take the place of therapy for those with more serious problems, but it can also be a helpful adjunct to treatment for therapists working with adolescents.

I hope you will enjoy—and benefit from—taking the action-mindset journey.

—Carlo DiClemente, PhD
Emeritus professor of psychology,
University of Maryland—Baltimore County
Developer with James Prochaska of the
transtheoretical stages of change model

A NOTE TO MY FELLOW THERAPISTS AND HELPING PROFESSIONALS

We all know that one's power and a healthy self-esteem lie in taking the initiative in life and being proactive rather than passive or reactive. The question, though, is how to get teens (and others) to change their deeply ingrained habit of avoiding people and situations that make them fearful; how to get them to tolerate the distress that comes with stepping outside their comfort zones and move in the direction of sustained effort to achieve what they value and what matters to them.

The organization of this book was inspired by an approach that I have found works pretty reliably over my many years as a practitioner. I believe this book can help you work successfully with individual teens and groups in a clinical, classroom, or other setting.

Applying a transtheoretical model, I first explain in easily understood terms why making change can be difficult and the stages of change teens can expect to go through on the way to success. That, in combination with elements of ACT (exploration of values), positive psychology (conveying the possibility of optimism, hope), seeking buy-in through motivational interviewing (asking how you would like tomorrow to be different from today), and a focus on how to achieve distress tolerance, set a foundation for therapy—teens' understanding of the purpose of CBT strategies in treatment—before the strategies are introduced. This workbook provides a road map for helping teens begin that process and sustain the effort to develop an action mindset. A progress-measuring tool that we call the Get Ready!-Get Set!-Go! Meter can be used to assess and monitor fluctuations in motivation and progress in taking action for every session or as needed.

Over the past several years, and especially while writing this book and creating corresponding activities, I have developed a CBT for Anxiety curriculum that I adapt for use with both middle schoolers and high schoolers. It can be implemented virtually, in person, or in a hybrid format. Here is an example of an eight-session program for teens:

1. **Getting acquainted.** This session involves discussing values, goals, and motivation for making what teens feel is an important improvement or change.

2. **Basics of CBT and the importance of being able to tolerate uncertainty and discomfort.** This session includes a review of possible rewards to increase motivation.

3. **Overcoming the obstacles of problematic thinking habits and bodily sensations.** Teens select two negative thinking habits explored in *Conquer Negative Thinking for Teens: A Workbook to Break the Nine Thought Habits That Are Holding You Back*, and complete the activities in the relevant chapters over a week or two (Alvord and McGrath 2017).

4. **Continued exploration of thinking habits that get in the way**

5. **Setting up an anxiety hierarchy and developing an anxiety exposure staircase**

6. **Starting at the first step of the exposure staircase, practicing and discussing their actions**

7. **Continued steps on the exposure staircase.** For those who tend to depression, a behavioral activation planner is introduced.

8. **Consideration of which strategies or tools teens have found to be most useful.** This includes writing or drawing an image of them in their toolkit (see chapter 10) and discussion of how they will continue progressing toward their goal.

This curriculum is easily adaptable and can be spread over more sessions as needed. I hope you will find these ideas—and the discussion and exercises in this workbook—to be useful in your clinical work.

—Mary K. Alvord, PhD

INTRODUCTION

If you're reading these words, the chances are good that you—like pretty much all teens everywhere—frequently find yourself bombarded by a storm of changing emotions and struggling with painful feelings of worry, insecurity, and self-doubt. These ups and downs are a normal result of spreading your wings, facing new academic and social challenges, and claiming greater independence. The opportunities you are gaining to shape your own future—and the responsibility you have to do so—can leave you exhilarated one day and paralyzed with panic the next.

Though such tumult is expected during this time of growth, a big problem arises when your emotions and insecurities cause you to say no to opportunities—even when saying yes would help you reach goals that matter to you and make you happier. Many teens handle self-doubt and worry and sadness by avoiding people and situations that intimidate them, rather than stepping outside their comfort zone to try new things and accept new challenges. But as we'll see, while withdrawing to the sidelines of your life may offer relief in the short run, in the long run it generally leads only to disappointment, discouragement, and even more deeply entrenched anxiety and sadness. And thriving in your endeavors as you go through life has much to do with being proactive, meaning taking the initiative to *make things happen* rather than sitting back passively and cautiously to *wait and see what happens*.

This workbook is designed to help you make the crucial and highly rewarding journey from avoidance to action and proactivity. The discussion and practice exercises in each chapter will help you understand and overcome the fears that are holding you back and guide you in developing one of your greatest superpowers: an action mindset.

Why do we call this a superpower? Because you have the ability—right now!—to influence what happens next in your life, and the extent to which you will thrive in school and in your relationships. You can take steps today that will increase your confidence and raise your odds of happiness next week and next year as they advance you on the path you envision for yourself. Maybe you love soccer or playing the trumpet, and that path leads you to trying out for a community team or a concert solo. Maybe it leads to joining freely in school activities as a way to expand your circle of friends.

The guidance and strategies we offer are based on the principles of *cognitive behavioral therapy*, or CBT. Research in this branch of psychology has shown that our thoughts, emotions, bodily sensations, and actions are highly interdependent—in other words, each has a major impact on the others.

As you'll see, for example, faulty negative thinking patterns (*I'm such a loser!*; *They'll think I'm dumb!*) are often what undermine teens' self-confidence and freeze them in their tracks, preventing them from trying out for that team or solo performance or from going to social events. Similarly, mistakes we make and the embarrassment we suffer when we do take action influence the way we think about ourselves and our world. The unpleasant physical sensations that are triggered by worries and anxiety, such as nausea and a racing heart, often affect our behavior and our thinking (*I can't do it!*; *I might throw up in public!*). Flawed thinking, and the actions that we take (or don't take), directly influence our mood too. And our mood affects the way we think and behave.

The flip side of that—and the message of this book—is that you can change your thinking and behavior patterns in helpful ways, influencing the way you feel. Developing more realistic and positive thinking habits (*I'm smart, I can try; Everybody makes mistakes!*) can give you the shot of courage you need to take actions you've wanted to take but haven't out of worry or fear. And cultivating an action mindset by taking steps even when you're scared offers the glow of accomplishment as you get closer and closer to where you want to end up. Keep in mind that tiny steps are fine. They'll contribute to your growing sense of confidence as you gain ground.

Changing any ingrained habit is not easy, of course. It requires commitment and, as you'll discover when you tackle the exercises in each chapter, it takes practice. We've devoted much of chapter 3 to exploring the process you'll go through as you work your way through this book and turn that avoidance habit into an action mindset. The process will take you from the stage in which you're preparing to change your behavior pattern (we call this stage Get Ready!) through the planning stage, in which you figure out what steps to take (Get Set!) to the point at which you take the plunge and get moving (Go!).

One of the key steps in the Get Ready! stage, for example, is to think through *why* you want to make that change. What do you value in life that makes overcoming your avoidance habit worthwhile? Maybe it's your passion for sports or photography or a strong desire for close friendships. What do you think might happen if you act? How would your life be different next week or in six months or in a year? How might your friendships and family relationships improve?

While withdrawing and avoiding other people and situations are very common coping strategies for teens, the underlying contributors to an avoidance habit differ. For this reason, we explore the main causes (and strategies for overcoming them) in separate chapters. You can work your way through all of them if you like, or focus on the chapters that resonate most strongly.

Often, for instance, a need to avoid and withdraw springs from chronic worry about what the future holds and what the outcome of an action might be (probably something awful!). Or if you're a perfectionist, and anything less than total success is unacceptable, choosing not to risk slipping up is often the most appealing path. Social anxiety is a widely shared obstacle to action; it shows up in some teens as acute discomfort when interacting with other people and in some as paralyzing self-consciousness when they're expected to be the center of attention or perform for an audience. Sadness and depression are frequent causes too. When you're feeling really down, it can be tough to resist the appeal of hiding out alone in your room.

By the time you've finished this book, you'll have accumulated a number of tried-and-true tools for your action-mindset toolkit—strategies you can use to help yourself be brave and get moving. Among the most important, which you'll use again and again, are the strategies that can help you adjust to and begin to tolerate discomfort. A major impediment to taking chances and rising to new challenges is the anguish we experience, emotional and physical, when facing uncertain outcomes. That may be intense anxiety, for instance, or it may be bodily sensations such as nausea, dizziness, sweatiness, and a racing heart. Making small practice moves that psychologists call exposures is a proven way to gradually get used to uncomfortable feelings and reassure yourself that they aren't unbearable after all.

The good news is that the work you do on this journey is likely to pay off in a major way. We hope that you arrive at a belief in, and appreciation for, the power you have to shape your future in profound ways—and a sense of anticipation and excitement about engaging fully in the adventure ahead.

CHAPTER 1

ARE YOU LIVING YOUR LIFE ON THE SIDELINES?

Understand What Is Holding You Back
and How to Move Forward

FOR YOU TO KNOW

IF YOU'RE LIKE MOST TEENS, you're acutely aware of the ways that worry, anxiety, fear, self-doubt, and feelings of sadness and insecurity negatively affect your quality of life. Too often, these feelings prevent teens from getting out there and doing the things they would like to do or from solving a problem that is holding them back.

In fact, avoidance of difficult situations and emotions, and withdrawal from contact with other people, are very common coping responses in people of all ages when they face situations that make them anxious or when they are weighed down by sadness or depression. Such actions—or more accurately, decisions *not* to act—are understandable, because in that particular moment they feel good. They help relieve the fears or added pressure and stress that we're experiencing. But beyond that moment of relief, they often make us feel worse. And deciding not to act just reinforces the belief that we can't cope with our fears.

Do any of the following scenarios sound familiar? If so, you're not alone.

- You love to sing (or run or play basketball) and wish you had the nerve to try out for a role in the school musical (or a spot on the track or basketball team). But as the big day approaches, you become more and more fearful of freezing up and looking dumb in front of your peers. Better not risk it, you think, as you skip tryouts and head home. The next day, you feel angry at yourself for being too scared to try.

- You and your sister are wandering through the mall when you spot a group of your classmates eating and laughing together in the food court. You wish you had the confidence to go over and join the group. Your sister says she'll come back and pick you up later if you want to stay, but you hurry off with her, pretending not to notice them. It would be too embarrassing to break into the conversation—especially if it's possible they wouldn't want you to join in. Later, you feel really bummed that you're no good at making friends.

- A girl you like recently had a date with someone else, and you've been feeling sad and really down on yourself for the past few weeks. When your cousin invites you to come with a group of his friends to a Halloween party, you say no. It's much more appealing to hole up at home and play video games than to try making conversation with a bunch of people you don't know. But spending the evening shut up in your room alone just makes you feel lonelier and more down.

- You have a big group history project due at the end of the week that is going to require you to give a class presentation on the long-term effects of the Allied victory in World War II. Your team is counting on you to deliver an A. Problem is, you don't have a good grasp of the material and you haven't started writing yet. You figure you'll get yourself off the hook by staying home sick that day.

THE PROBLEM WITH THE AVOIDANCE HABIT

What happens longer term when you regularly give in to the tendency to dodge the challenges you face and stick to the sidelines in life? Your anxieties and insecurities tend to become even stronger when you decline to face them and back away rather than move forward in spite of your discomfort. Avoidance becomes a habit. And the result of constantly avoiding taking risks is that you bypass the many opportunities that present themselves to enjoy your life to the fullest and to make progress toward realizing your goals and dreams.

You miss out. Missing out on the fun of being part of a team or of meeting new people, for instance, often leads to even deeper feelings of sadness and loneliness, as well as a profound sense of disappointment in yourself.

The purpose of this workbook is to help you understand that choosing to act and problem solve, even when you'd rather not, is one of your greatest superpowers when it comes to thriving in school and life. Action opens the path to new ways of fully engaging in your life. And many teens like yourself have already discovered that taking even a couple of small steps can actually be a great way to get a handle on all those fears and doubts, and to lift a gloomy mood.

Breaking that habit of avoidance and instead developing what we can think of as an *action mindset* can give you an exhilarating sense of your capabilities, and a realistic sense of optimism and hope about what your future holds. You won't always land the role in the play or the spot on the team, of course. And you may not always be able to earn an A on a challenging assignment. But it's important to remember that putting in the effort when a goal is really important to you is in itself a form of success.

HOW MIGHT THIS WORK?

Suppose you're the teen in the first example above, paralyzed with anxiety at the thought of coming in last in a race during tryouts for the track team. To work up the courage to give it a shot anyway, you might start by imagining how much fun you could have as part of the team. Maybe you decide to watch a practice to get a sense of what the drills are like, and then ask a friend to time you while you run sprints.

Finally, you might consider what would happen if you did come in last, and ask yourself whether the risks are worth it. Yes, you might feel embarrassed for a day or two, and definitely disappointed at not making the team. But it took guts to set a goal and go for it. And being able to congratulate yourself for trying often feels great.

YOUR THOUGHTS, BEHAVIOR, BODY SENSATIONS, AND MOOD

What we imagine to be true and what we tell ourselves about what's going to happen and what has happened make a huge difference in how fearful or willing we are to take action. The recognition that our thoughts and behavior are intimately dependent on each other, and that both greatly affect our body sensations and mood, is the guiding principle of a branch of psychology called *cognitive behavioral therapy* (CBT).

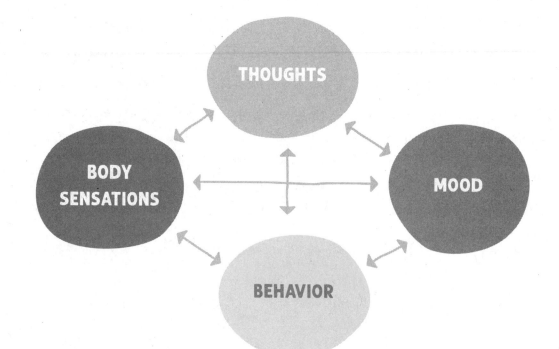

CBT teaches that questioning your unrealistic, off-target negative thought patterns (that unfriendly voice in your head shouting *I'm such a loser!* and *I can't do this!*) and substituting more realistic, helpful thoughts can have an impact on what you do, or don't do. And it's an important step in improving your mood. Very often, in fact, it's that hurtful unrealistic self-talk that freezes teens in their tracks.

Identifying and examining the truth of these thoughts is often a key step in calming those worries and finding the nerve to act. We explore in detail how to challenge unrealistic thoughts in *Conquer Negative Thinking for Teens: A Workbook to Break the Nine Thought Habits That Are Holding You Back* (Alvord and McGrath 2017).

BECOMING AWARE OF SIGNALS FROM YOUR BODY

Sometimes, anxious teens avoid situations because they expect intolerable bodily sensations to kick in—nausea, panicky breathing, profuse sweating, and a racing heart, for example. It seems preferable to skip school rather than face giving an oral presentation in English class when you predict that you'll feel sick to your stomach and possibly even throw up in public. You might make excuses not to join a group of classmates for pizza if you assume that you'll say something embarrassing and break out in a sweat. The following chapters will help you begin to tolerate and even accept such sensations and understand that they aren't dangerous.

Likewise, changing your usual avoidance response by deciding to take a brave positive step *in spite of* your hard-to-tame negative thoughts or upset stomach can affect the way you think about yourself and your potential, calm your anxiety, and give your mood a boost.

These strategies have helped many teens become more willing to take risks, more open to new relationships, and just plain happier. Putting them to work in your own life won't be easy. Experts have long known that altering ingrained behavior patterns is extremely difficult—witness all the examples of even superconfident adults who resolve to work out every day and regularly stick to the couch. But remember: no pain, no gain! In chapter 3, we'll explore the ingredients and process of making change successfully. The rest of the workbook will give you practice at taking a deep breath and diving into all sorts of situations.

★ ★ ★ FOR YOU TO DO ★ ★ ★

The activities that follow will help you better understand a fundamental principle of CBT: how your thoughts, body sensations, behavior, and mood are all interdependent and influence each other. The goal is that you'll begin to see what it is that makes you want to avoid taking an action or steer clear of other people or situations. Having that awareness can often help you decide to move at least a couple of small steps in the direction you'd like to go.

The first exercise presents a number of negative thinking habits that distort what is really true and are very common in teens (and in people of all ages). It asks you to consider whether any of these habits have caused you to bypass an opportunity and stick to the sidelines. Think back over times you've felt stuck recently. Can you recognize any instances when such off-target thinking has caused you to choose inaction even when you've wished you had the confidence to act? Two additional activities will explore specific ways that thoughts affect actions (and vice versa) and how both impact the body and mood.

Which of These Thinking Habits Keep You from Taking Action?

Negative thinking habits that distort reality are very common causes of the insecurities and sadness that cause teens to flee or feel paralyzed. Put a check next to the habits that sometimes keep you from taking action. In the space provided, describe a situation in which a specific thought caused you *not* to act.

 THE "I CAN'T!" HABIT. When you're faced with a new challenge or a tough problem, you automatically tell yourself that you're not capable of meeting the challenge or solving the problem. This lack of confidence often makes you give up before you even try and feel anxious and sad.

 THE CATASTROPHIZING HABIT. You often expect disaster when you're faced with uncertainty and imagine all sorts of gloom-and-doom scenarios. You spend a lot of time feeling needlessly panicky and frozen with anxiety.

 THE ALL-OR-NOTHING HABIT. You see situations in extremes. For example, if your performance isn't perfect, it's a total failure. Or any event that doesn't happen one "right" way is all wrong. This makes you feel down on yourself or upset and irritated with others, and you're apt to give up.

THE ZOOMING-IN-ON-THE-NEGATIVE HABIT. You get stuck thinking over and over about your disappointing or embarrassing experiences and filter out everything positive or even just neutral that also happened. Blowing the negative moments way out of proportion results in pessimism about the present and future and can often lead to depression and withdrawal.

 THE "I SHOULD, YOU SHOULD" HABIT. You hold yourself or other people to a set of rigid and unreasonable rules. When events unfold in ways that don't meet your expectations, you feel disappointed in yourself or frustrated with others. Either way, you're not in a frame of mind to take a positive step.

 THE FORTUNE-TELLING HABIT. You jump to the conclusion that you're certainly going to mess up or that a future event will be a disappointment. You tend to get really down on yourself and feel either unmotivated and depressed, or cheated and resentful.

 THE MIND-READING HABIT. Even in situations when it isn't possible to tell what someone else is thinking, you jump to the conclusion that the person is thinking about you in an unfriendly, critical way. This makes you want to avoid the person, and you feel anxious or sad.

THE BLAMING HABIT. When a mistake is made or something undesirable happens, you either think, *It's all my fault!* (and feel guilty or down on yourself) or *It's all their fault!* (and feel angry and resentful). In either case, you throw up your hands and don't take any action in response.

 THE "IT'S NOT FAIR!" HABIT. You get upset when you feel that you've been unjustly treated, even though fairness is an unrealistic expectation. Or you feel mad that you're being told to do something you don't think is fair.

Can you see yourself in any of these examples of negative, unrealistic thinking? Becoming aware of your faulty self-talk allows you to catch those off-target thoughts whenever they enter your head and to pause for a **REALITY CHECK**. What is a more realistic way of looking at the situation? When you consider what is most likely to be true, you often gain the confidence to take a positive step forward.

See How Behavior Is Linked to Thoughts and Mood

Now let's look more closely at how thoughts and mood and behavior affect each other, and how reframing our thoughts can give us the boost we need to take action. First, consider the example of Carlos, who is thinking about trying out for the soccer team. Look at the ways his decision is influenced by what he thinks and feels, physically and emotionally. How can he reframe his thoughts so they're more realistic? Then add your own ideas of what steps he could take to make it possible to go to the tryouts.

CARLOS loves to play soccer with his friends and would like to be on their city-league team. He wants to try out next month but, remembering all the goofs he's made when playing just for fun, he worries that he won't make the cut. It's important for Carlos to be aware of his thoughts, mood, physical sensations, and actions. Understanding his hesitancy to show up at tryouts will help him take some steps to get there.

I'm too slow and not good enough at moving the ball. It's hopeless! If I try out, I'll just be embarrassed, so why bother?

A more helpful thought: *It's not hopeless; I can practice before tryouts. And there's no chance of being on the team if I don't try out. So I really want to do it!*

- Worried
- A little sad
- Conflicted: excited about the possibility of making the team but anxious about trying out

HIS THOUGHTS

HIS BODY SENSATIONS

HIS MOOD

HIS BEHAVIOR

- *Tight stomach*
- *Fast breathing*
- *Shaky legs*

He hesitates to take the chance of failing and is leaning toward skipping tryouts.

What steps can Carlos take to make trying out possible? Add your own ideas on the blank lines.

1. Imagine himself having fun playing on the team with his friends.

2. Practice his soccer skills.

3. _____

_____

Do you see how Carlos's reality check (*It's not hopeless—I can practice*) leads to helpful action? Let's look at how this process might work for you.

Tell Your Own Story

In the space below, briefly describe a situation from your own life when you wanted to try something new or go to a social event but opted not to because you were fearful or feeling down.

_____

_____

_____

_____

_____

_____

_____

_____

_____

_____

_____

Next, fill in the blanks in the diagram. Note the thoughts preventing you from taking action, a more helpful thought, your body sensations and mood, and how you behaved as a result. Jot down a few steps you might have taken instead that would have helped you reach your goal—and that you can take if you're faced with a similar situation in the future.

A more helpful thought: _____

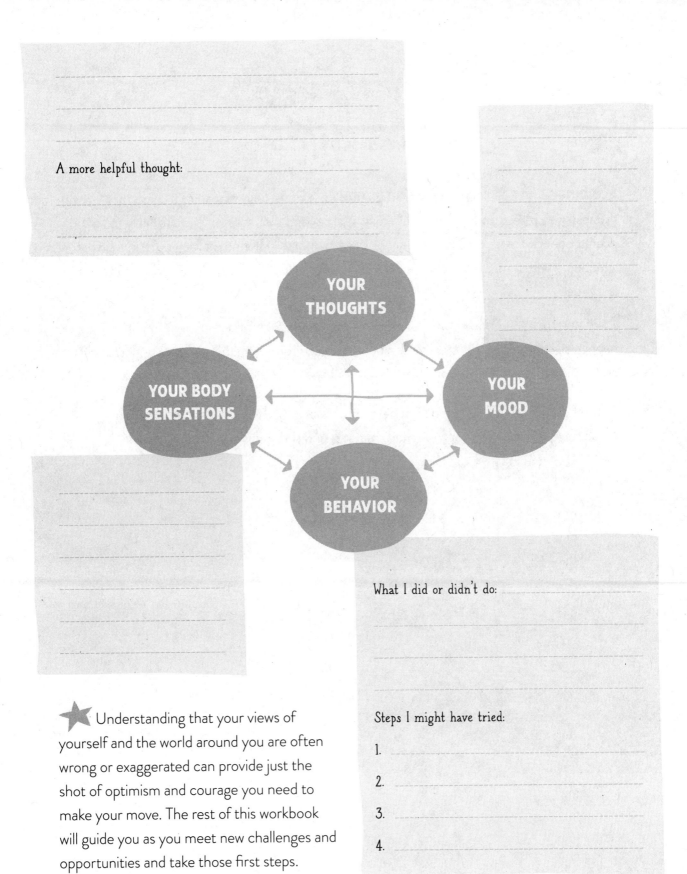

YOUR
THOUGHTS

YOUR BODY
SENSATIONS

YOUR
MOOD

YOUR
BEHAVIOR

What I did or didn't do: _____

Steps I might have tried:

1. _____

2. _____

3. _____

4. _____

⭐ Understanding that your views of yourself and the world around you are often wrong or exaggerated can provide just the shot of optimism and courage you need to make your move. The rest of this workbook will guide you as you meet new challenges and opportunities and take those first steps.

KEY TAKEAWAYS

AVOIDING PEOPLE OR CHALLENGING SITUATIONS out of feelings of insecurity, fear, or sadness may relieve your immediate stress. But beyond that moment, you're likely to feel even more down and worried and disappointed in yourself. The next time you're in a similar situation, your anxiety is apt to be even more powerful because you didn't face it and fight it last time.

Choosing to act, even when you're reluctant to, is an important component of achieving happiness and success as you grow. It opens the door to a rich variety of new opportunities and experiences, and leads you to more fully engage in your life.

Our off-target self-talk is often what gets in the way of action. It's possible to examine those thoughts and come up with more realistic, and thus helpful, substitutes.

CHAPTER 2

YOUR GOAL

Develop the Habit of

Being Proactive

As we've discussed, if you get the urge to hide out and avoid taking action when you're feeling insecure, anxious, or sad, you're not alone. One explanation for why this urge is so common is that many teens who often feel insecure and unhappy share a sense of helplessness and hopelessness—they believe that they lack the ability to influence what happens in a given situation. But avoiding action, while it may remove the risk of failure or embarrassment in the moment, often leads to a greater sense of helplessness and hopelessness in the longer run. And you may grow even more fearful or disappointed in yourself.

A key goal of this workbook is to help you quash the faulty notion that you're a helpless victim. We'll help you recognize the capacity you have to make a difference in the way events unfold, and to tap into that power by developing the habit of taking a proactive approach to life. What does that mean exactly?

People who are proactive believe they can have an impact on what happens today and in the future. They are optimistic about their future. Rather than sit back and wait to see what unfolds, they grab opportunities to work toward the results they want.

Instead of moping around the house complaining of boredom on a snowy Saturday, for example, proactive teens might text a friend to come over and bake brownies or play video games or go sledding. Like good drivers on the lookout for danger down the road, proactive people also are alert for problems looming ahead, and they look for ways to either head off trouble or find a fix.

Being proactive won't always get you a great outcome on the first try. But it *will* give you a much better chance of success and satisfaction than you'll get by simply staying in your room while you hope for the best. And as you practice taking action, it will begin to become a habit.

It's true, of course, that you can't control everything in your path, but you have a lot more ability to influence events than you probably think. And choosing to determine the directions your life takes feels really, really empowering! In fact, psychologists have shown that *self-efficacy*, or the belief in your ability to take action and make a difference in what happens to you, is one of the key characteristics of people who are resilient. This means they are better able to adapt to disappointments and hardships and bounce back from difficulties with hope and optimism.

BEING PROACTIVE VS. BEING PASSIVE OR REACTIVE

Suppose you have a big math exam coming up in a few days, and you're totally confused about sorting and classifying rational and irrational numbers. You're starting to panic, because you really need a good grade on the test to stay in B territory. But you're shy, and way too nervous to ask the math whiz who sits behind you for an explanation. And you're worried that if you go in after class to ask for extra help, your teacher will get mad that you've waited this long. With time to study quickly running out, how would you handle this situation?

 A PROACTIVE MOVE would be to recognize that you have control over whether or not you go in to the test understanding rational and irrational numbers. Next, you would muster the courage to tackle the problem and consult another student or your teacher as soon as possible. Sure, your teacher might be a little annoyed that you waited until the last minute—or maybe you'll get credit for caring enough to ask. And you'll be able to take pride in knowing that you did your best to get ready for the exam.

 A PASSIVE MOVE would be to tell yourself that it's too late to make a difference and take the test without getting any help. You'd hope for the best and wait to see what happens.

A big downside of taking the passive path is that, instead of influencing events and the outcome, you're forced to be *reactive*. That means you simply react to whatever happens. If the difficult concepts turn out to be a small part of the test and you get a good grade in spite of being passive, great—you can react by celebrating. But frequently when we just let events happen, we don't like the outcome at all and feel frustrated and disappointed that we didn't take action. A bad grade on the test might cause you to react with annoyance or anger at yourself or your teacher, or with shame or discouragement.

SHARPEN YOUR SKILLS

Luckily, behaving proactively, and developing an ability to anticipate and head off problems, are skills you can work on and improve. As you turn these behaviors into a habit, they become automatic—and much less anxiety producing. Here are a few key messages you can give yourself as you practice becoming a more proactive person:

✓ **IN MOST SITUATIONS, WE HAVE SOME CONTROL.** Okay, it's true that if your mom gets transferred to a job in a different city, you're probably not going to be able to refuse to move. But even in situations like this where your control is limited, you can take steps that will ease the pain of the move. In other words, you can control how you respond, and influence the outcome. Think about what's really bothering you. Are you worried that you won't have any friends at your new school? You absolutely have the power to do something about that. Maybe there will be an orientation before classes start where you can meet other kids who are new to the school. And perhaps you can join a team or a club.

✓ **STUMBLES ARE OKAY.** Getting better at being proactive requires allowing the possibility that you'll make mistakes and fail sometimes. It's important to remember that missteps and failures are a fact of life, and that trial and error are often a key part of the way progress is made. Your favorite pro athletes and musicians almost certainly messed up multiple times on their way to success, and just kept trying again or correcting their course. You can think of your stumbles as opportunities to grow and learn from experience.

✓ **A CHALLENGE ISN'T ALWAYS JUST AN OBSTACLE.** Many teens feel overwhelmed and helpless and freeze or flee when they face a problem or challenge, such as an assignment to complete a big group project for a class in the next week. It can help to think of challenges as opportunities, as a call to action. Rather than insurmountable obstacles, challenges are situations calling for creative ways to find solutions and gain ground. How might you and the other members of the group divide up the research and writing responsibilities to get the project done on time? Perhaps you can suggest getting together after school or setting up a video call to figure it out.

★ ★ ★ FOR YOU TO DO ★ ★ ★

Your goal as you face new challenges and opportunities in school and life will be to consider how you might act to improve the odds of getting the results you want. In any given situation, what does it look like to behave proactively? Passively? The exercises that follow will give you a better understanding of the difference, and a greater appreciation for the power of proactivity.

Proactive or Passive?

Read the following scenarios. Put a check in the column at right that indicates whether a scenario illustrates a proactive or a passive response.

SITUATION	PROACTIVE	PASSIVE
I want to expand my circle of friends. I hope that Max calls me this week.		
This math homework is really hard. I'll worry about it later.		
My sister came home from school upset. I'll ask her what's wrong and figure out if I can help.		
Talia's parents can no longer drive us to the mall on Saturday. I'll find us another ride.		
Mila seemed mad at me today. Maybe she'll text me tonight.		
I'll use my time on social media to connect with more people.		
I like playing soccer in gym so much that I've signed up for a local league.		

Choose one of the illustrations of passive behavior above and describe the likely outcome. Then, imagine a more proactive approach that probably would produce better results.

_____

_____

_____

_____

⭐ Next, let's look more closely at how you can turn your impulse to passively hang back into much more fruitful action. Remember: You have more power than you think!

Find Your Power

People who are proactive believe in their self-efficacy, their power to improve the odds that they'll reach their goals and deal with any obstacles that crop up along the way. To get a sense of how teens can develop their own feelings of self-efficacy, consider Keisha's story and answer the questions that follow.

Several girls in **KEISHA'S** *Saturday morning dance class regularly get together afterward to share a pizza or go see a movie. Keisha, who has been good friends with two of the girls since middle school, would really like to join the group. But lately she feels nervous that her friends don't like her and might not even want to be friends anymore. They eat lunch with her most days and all ride the bus together, but when she sees them laughing and talking together in school, she often worries that they're talking about her and judging her in a negative way. Every Saturday, Keisha hopes that she'll be invited to go along with the group, but she hurries out of class rather than risk having her feelings hurt.*

Think about Keisha's behavior. In what way is she being passive?

_____

_____

_____

_____

As we discussed in chapter 1, it's often teens' critical self-talk that causes them to get stuck. How are Keisha's thoughts affecting how she feels and how she behaves? Are her thoughts realistic?

_____

_____

_____

_____

What proactive step or steps might Keisha take to improve the chances that she'll become friendly with the girls in her dance class and be able to join the fun after class?

_____

_____

_____

_____

Figuring out what she can do to influence what happens, and then doing it even when taking the risk is uncomfortable, gives Keisha a sense of empowerment. She learns that she is not helpless and _can_ take steps to get what she wants. Even if she doesn't get the results she hopes for and never ends up hanging out with this particular group after class, she now has a little more courage to be proactive in the future. She can tap her power to text or talk with other girls in the dance class or in school, for example, and invite someone to see a movie or sleep over. She can take the initiative in making and nurturing new friendships.

Create a Storyboard to Visualize Your Own Change

Now, think of a current situation in your own life in which you've tended to be passive, but that would definitely be improved if you were to try being proactive instead. In the boxes below, describe or draw the following scenes:

SCENE 1: Illustrate or describe how you are being passive now.

SCENE 2: Illustrate or describe one proactive step

you can take to improve the situation.

A small step is fine.

SCENE 3: Illustrate or describe what you hope
the outcome(s) will be if you take action. Think of this scene
as your new computer screen or phone wallpaper!

KEY TAKEAWAYS

MANY TEENS WHO OFTEN FEEL ANXIOUS OR UNHAPPY HAVE A HABIT of behaving passively because they believe they're helpless to have an impact on what occurs in a given situation. Or maybe they feel too hopeless to even try. Remember: You are not helpless! You obviously can't control everything that happens in your life, but you have a lot more power to influence events than you think. Create your proactive habit by seeing challenges as a call to action.

When you gain confidence in your self-efficacy, or your ability to proactively solve problems and influence the course your life takes, you become better able to adapt to disappointment and move ahead with hope and optimism.

This point bears repeating: Mistakes and failures are okay and to be expected. It's important to keep in mind that they're a natural and necessary part of learning and growing and making progress.

CHAPTER 3

GETTING READY TO ACT

Give Yourself a
Pep Talk

One of the toughest parts of being a teenager is that you're often going to be challenged to try new things, take new risks, and face uncertainty as you gain independence and make decisions about your own priorities and opportunities. There's a good reason that kind of risk-taking is often called stepping outside your comfort zone.

We all develop habits and coping strategies that allow us to feel safe in familiar territory in our daily lives. For example, an introverted adult finds a reason to skip a meeting, because going will probably mean having to offer ideas publicly to the group. Similarly, a teen who worries about not being smart or popular enough might avoid giving answers in class and never go to parties.

Changing those safe behaviors often involves choosing and being able to tolerate considerable discomfort. Reluctance to take that chance—the impulse that freezes you in your tracks and causes you to avoid sports tryouts or showing up awkwardly at a party—is a normal response common in people of all ages.

While changing such avoidance behavior by going outside your comfort zone can be really hard, the effort is likely to pay off in a big way:

✔ By seizing opportunities to pursue what is really important to you, you open the door to new adventures. You accept the chance to develop new interests and spend more satisfying time with friends. And you may develop new relationships that make you excited and happy.

✔ By taking a chance that you might look foolish or fail at something in the moment, you can experience the satisfaction of making progress toward your goals. Many hugely successful people, from tech billionaires to Olympic athletes, have discovered that trial and error—and making adjustments and trying again and again—are valuable, essential steps along the way.

Clearly, there's a big price to pay for saying no, and staying on the sidelines. This chapter will explore how to give yourself the courage and confidence—the pep talk—to take the plunge.

GET READY! GET SET! GO! HOW WE CHANGE

Two experts who study how people let go of unproductive habits and substitute positive behaviors, James Prochaska and Carlo DiClemente (1982), have identified several key stages of the change process that hold true for pretty much any kind of difficult change, from battling an addiction to nachos or vaping or video games to forming a homework-before-texting habit. Applying these principles when tackling your tendency to avoid uncomfortable situations can be very useful in building your confidence to take action instead. You'll learn how to do so as you work your way through this guide. The five key stages of change are:

1. **PRECONTEMPLATION.** At this point, the need to change is not yet clear. Anxious teens, for example, are secure and content in their comfort zones and have yet to realize that there are compelling reasons to venture outside those zones. The benefits of avoiding scary moves (like trying out for the school musical or joining a conversation with classmates at the mall) are still much more appealing than the scary moves. Because you're reading this book, you've most likely passed through this stage already.

2. **CONTEMPLATION.** Think of this as the Get Ready! stage. You can now see that you're probably hurting yourself by sticking with your old habits, but still are pondering whether the pain of changing is worthwhile. Yes, you think, it would be a lot of fun to be in the school musical and hang out with the rest of the cast at rehearsals. But the idea of performing a selection in front of all the competition is terrifying. You weigh the options: should you try out or skip it?

    Meantime, teens who tend to withdraw to their rooms when they feel really down and alone may have a suspicion that they're making their loneliness worse, but don't quite believe that simply taking an action can actually make them feel better. In this stage, you work toward a decision to change by asking yourself what is really important to you, and why. Psychologists call this process *motivational interviewing*, and you'll be reading more on this. Acknowledging that both music and strengthening your friendships are key to your happiness, for example, helps you decide that the possibilities offered by trying out are worth taking the risk.

3. **PREPARATION.** This is the planning stage, which we'll call Get Set! You've weighed the options and have decided you're ready to take a positive step in the near future. Now it's time to come up with your plan. What smart step or steps can you take that will move you toward the audition and a part in the play?

   Maybe you can ask your music teacher for some help practicing a song before tryouts. Then you can get a few friends together and do a run-through in front of an audience. One part of your preparation might be to remind yourself that stumbling now and then is a natural part of eventually succeeding. Maybe you'll be disappointed for a while if you don't make the cast, but you can be proud of having tried. And there will be other opportunities.

4. **ACTION.** Now you're ready to GO! This is when you take the steps you've committed to and start behaving in a new, more productive way. You get help from your music teacher, practice hard, and begin to realize that even the small steps can be exhilarating and empowering, helping you build confidence in your capabilities and feel more hopeful. If Plan A doesn't work, and you don't land a role, you can formulate a Plan B and a Plan C and try those. How about volunteering for the stage crew? The key is to change course rather than give up.

5. **MAINTENANCE.** What will you do the next time you're faced with a scary new challenge or find yourself in a social situation that makes you feel uncomfortable or sad and alone? Your goal now is to practice the skills you've developed in the contemplation, preparation, and action stages and build on your successes, however small. It's also important to reward yourself for your efforts, whether by treating yourself to an activity you enjoy or by simply pausing and taking pleasure in your accomplishment and the results.

HOW CAN THIS CHANGE PROCESS WORK FOR YOU?

As noted, this workbook assumes that you're already past the precontemplation stage—you've realized that there is value in acting and there are good reasons to stop avoiding any discomfort.

In the chapters that follow, we'll concentrate on helping you Get Ready!, Get Set!, and Go!— meaning move from contemplation (analyzing the problematic situation and figuring out why a change in your typical behavior is desirable) to planning (coming up with the steps you will take toward your goal) and finally to action (actually taking those steps). We'll also examine the rewards of taking action and how they can influence your choices going forward.

Many of the activities will focus on applying this process, and you'll be able to gauge your progress by plotting where you stand on a **READY!-SET!-GO! METER**, illustrated here. You can do that by shading in the meter as you move along or by drawing a figure or placing an X at your position, for example. Reaching the end of the meter means that you've reached your goal.

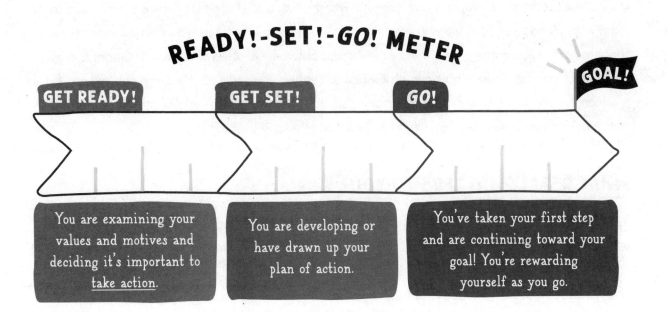

READY!-SET!-GO! METER

GET READY! **GET SET!** **GO!** **GOAL!**

You are examining your values and motives and deciding it's important to take action.

You are developing or have drawn up your plan of action.

You've taken your first step and are continuing toward your goal! You're rewarding yourself as you go.

Don't get discouraged if you don't make progress in a straight line. Remember, the process of change typically involves taking small steps in the direction you choose, sliding backward a few times, doing some replanning as needed, and then continuing to move forward. You might need to replot your position on the meter several times, in fact. That's completely normal and fine. You'll just have to be persistent and patient with yourself as you learn from making mistakes and keep trying to get it right.

UNHELPFUL THOUGHTS, HELPFUL THOUGHTS

As you begin the work of the contemplation stage, keep in mind that, as we explored in chapter 1, the anxieties, sadness, and insecurities that stop teens from taking a helpful action often stem from a steady flow of distorted, unhelpful self-talk running through their heads. Faced with a request to run for class treasurer, you think, *I can't do that—I'm not good at math!* and turn it down. Pondering whether to invite a new girl in your class to go with you to the movies, you think, *I'm too boring. She won't like me*, and watch TV by yourself instead.

Part of your task as you progress is to examine whether such off-target thinking is causing you to falter and say no to opportunities in your life. If so, you can practice catching yourself when these thoughts occur and coming up with more realistic, positive ways of viewing each situation: *It might be a lot of fun to be a class officer, and I know how to get help if I need it*; or *Reaching out to a new kid is a friendly thing to do, and she might be really glad*; or *Why assume she won't like me? She doesn't even know me yet.* These steps are what you practiced doing in chapter 1.

WHAT REALLY MATTERS TO YOU?

The exercises in this chapter will help you master another crucial Get Ready! step: identifying what truly is important to *you* (not your parents, not your friends). Research has demonstrated that reminding yourself what you value can be a good way to clarify why an action is needed (Hayes and Smith 2005). Our values are what we care deeply about, and they strongly influence how we want to spend our time and energies. For example, when you consider how much having good friends really matters to you, you may decide you don't want to skip the neighborhood barbecue after all. And taking the risk of inviting your new classmate to a movie may become more appealing.

Other examples of values include family, spirituality or religion, education, health, your passions (being an athlete or an artist or a scientist, say), and character traits such as honesty and integrity. If you especially value health and being an athlete, you're apt to be really disappointed if you say no to trying out for a community or school team. Someone who values integrity might feel that it's urgent to speak up when a wrong needs to be righted.

HOW DO YOU MOTIVATE YOURSELF TO TAKE ACTION?

Remembering what your values are gives you the big picture on why taking action is a good choice. But getting motivated to overcome your reluctance and actually do something in a specific situation can require an additional boost. Whenever you find yourself tempted to say no to action, it can be valuable to have the conversation with yourself known as motivational interviewing.

MOTIVATIONAL INTERVIEWING is a process developed by two psychologists, William Miller and Stephen Rollnick (2012), and used in therapy that helps people face and set aside their doubts or conflicted feelings. The idea is that, by asking yourself certain questions, you get inspired to act by more clearly seeing why an action is desirable and visualizing what the positive outcome might be.

For example, you might ask yourself:

- Why is changing my usual avoidance behavior important to me?

- How important is it on a 0–10 scale?

- What do I want tomorrow to be like?

- What will happen if I act differently than I normally would?

- What will happen if I don't?

You'll get the hang of examining what your own values and motives are when you complete the exercises that follow.

33

★ ★ ★ FOR YOU TO DO ★ ★ ★

Figuring out the answers to such questions about your motives can make all the difference when your fears and doubts and sadness stand in the way of action. (To sustain that motivation over time, you'll need other sources of strength as well, such as a nourishing diet and plenty of sleep.) The practice exercises here will guide you to a sense of what is most important to you, and a better understanding of how action will enhance the quality of your life. What do many teens discover when they examine how much taking a scary chance might add to their satisfaction and happiness? They find that the risk of taking the chance is less scary than they thought, and that the cost of avoiding action is too great.

What Do You Value?

Our values help guide the choices we make in our lives by defining what is most important to us. Identifying and giving weight to our values, a process often used in CBT, can help inspire us to take action. This exercise will help you identify your values.

First, read the following example for a sense of Sofia's values and how they influence her to move toward action.

Sofia values her family, friends, and health; her studies and extracurricular activities; and her creativity. Specifically, what matters most to her are her parents, having more than one good friend, getting enough sleep, dancing, and getting good grades in school. She realizes that being so shy is causing her to avoid interacting with new people at school and even making her hesitate to suggest get-togethers with classmates she does know. She decides that what she really wants to focus on now is reaching out more and feeling more comfortable around a small group of other teens. She makes a plan to start by asking the friendly girl who sits next to her in math class if she's going to the soccer game after school.

Next, check the boxes next to the values that are important to you. Fill in the blanks with specific examples that you find most meaningful.

RECREATION: _____

ARTS/MUSIC: _____

CHARACTER TRAITS (for example, integrity, honesty, perseverance): _____

_____

FAMILY: _____

FRIENDSHIP(S): _____

ACADEMIC ACHIEVEMENT: _____

○ PHYSICAL ACTIVITY: _____

○ INDEPENDENCE: _____

○ CREATIVITY, THINKING OUTSIDE THE BOX: _____

_____

○ RELIGION, SPIRITUALITY: _____

○ ADVENTURE/TRAVEL: _____

○ FUN: _____

○ HEALTH: _____

○ NATURE: _____

○ INNER PEACE: _____

○ OTHER: _____

Which of these values are most important to you? Take a look at Sofia's pie chart. Then, fill in your own pie chart on the next page so that the size of each slice represents how important that value is to you.

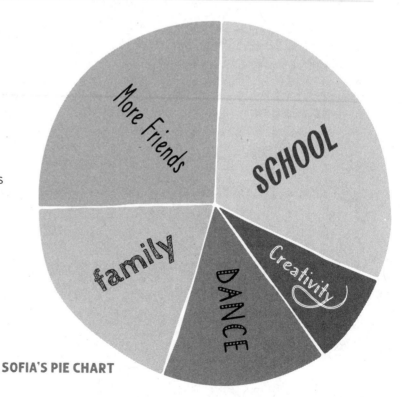

SOFIA'S PIE CHART

Now fill in your pie chart. Consider which values are most likely to influence you to *want* to act.

MY PIE CHART

⭐ Next, let's consider how identifying what appeals to you about taking action can motivate you to overcome your reluctance and take the leap.

Motivate Yourself!

GET READY! Think of an experience in your life when you avoided a situation or person, or you wanted to act but decided to stay in your comfort zone. Maybe you were anxious about failing or too depressed to have the energy and desire to act. Imagine that you're facing that same situation now. Asking yourself a series of questions such as these helps you consider what's important to *you* and can inspire you to make a difference in your life.

First, describe the experience briefly.

_____

_____

_____

What am I avoiding?

_____

_____

What does avoiding action keep me from doing or feeling?

_____

_____

Why is deciding to act important to me?

_____

_____

_____

How important is taking this step on a 0–10 scale? Circle your answer.

0   1   2   3   4   5   6   7   8   9   10

What will happen if I act differently than I normally would?

_____

_____

_____

If I don't act, what is likely to happen?

_____

_____

How does my avoidance behavior impact the people I care about?

_____

_____

_____

How will tomorrow be different if I take this step?

_____

_____

How might my life be different next month or next year?

_____

_____

_____

How hard will it really be to take this step?

_____

_____

_____

Do I feel confident that I can take small steps toward my goal?

_____

_____

_____

If I act, how would it make me feel about myself?

_____

_____

_____

If I act, what is the worst thing that might happen? The best thing?

_____

_____

_____

_____

⭐ Now let's look at the way that paying attention to your values can help you decide what change you want to make to your usual behavior and how to go about it.

Translate Your Values into an Action Plan

How do you translate your own values and motivations into a plan of action? For a sense of how the process works, read about Daniel's situation and note how he moves from understanding what he values and how action would benefit him to a concrete plan of doable steps.

GET READY! Daniel has identified that he really values playing his guitar and wants to find some friends who also play. He would love to join a band outside of school. He enjoys spending a lot of time practicing, but he is unsure whether he is good enough and is afraid he will be rejected. Further, he feels really shy about reaching out to people he doesn't know. So far, he has been playing it safe, practicing by himself, but that makes him feel sad and lonely. He has decided that playing with a band is important enough to him that he needs to figure out a way to make it happen.

GET SET! Next, Daniel formulates a plan of action based on his values and goal.

DANIEL'S VALUE	HIS GOAL	ACTIONABLE STEPS
Play music with a group	Stop playing only by himself; try out for a band	1. Play his guitar for someone in his family.
		2. Ask around to find bands that might need a guitar player.
		3. Call the bands to see if they are looking for someone.
		4. Ask if he could jam with them to be considered for the spot.
		5. Practice beforehand with a friend and possibly in front of several people.

 GO! Once he has a plan, Daniel begins taking one step at a time.

Now, you try it.

 Think back to the experience you described in activity 8. Reread what you wrote about why making a change is important to you.

GET SET! Next, complete the steps below using Daniel's example as a guide.

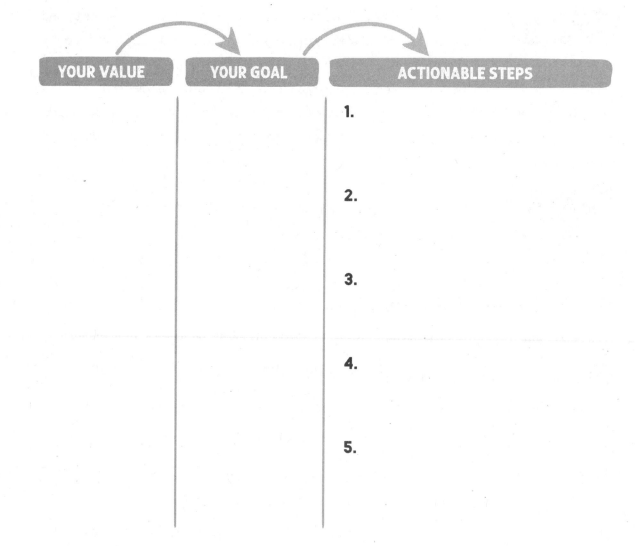

YOUR VALUE	YOUR GOAL	ACTIONABLE STEPS
		1.
		2.
		3.
		4.
		5.

Take the plunge! Remember, small—even tiny!—steps are fine.

Now, use your **READY!-SET!-GO! METER** to visualize your progress. You can indicate your position on the meter—anywhere from just beginning to "Get Set!" to hitting your goal—by shading in the bar, drawing a line or smiley face, or just by making a check. Keep in mind that backsliding and trying again are normal, essential parts of gaining ground, and you might have to take a step or two backward along the way. So it wouldn't hurt to use pencil!

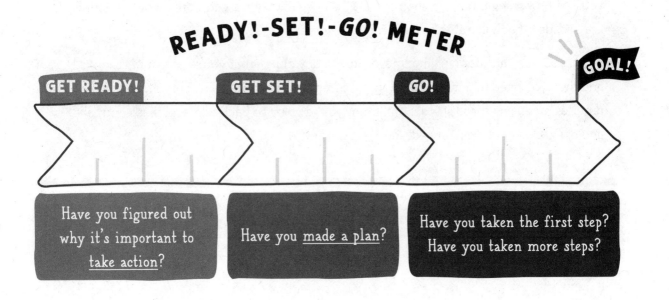

Download a blank Ready!-Set!-Go! Meter at http://www.newharbinger.com/50461.

KEY TAKEAWAYS

CHANGING ALL SORTS OF INGRAINED HABITS IS TOUGH FOR EVERYONE, so you're not alone. Teens who regularly avoid people or situations out of anxiety or sadness may struggle with changing that behavior because it means having to accept risk and tolerate discomfort. But the payoff of developing an action mindset is that you may greatly improve your happiness in the long run by opening the way to new experiences, new relationships, unexpected opportunities, and a sense of your own capabilities.

Identifying your personal values and your motives for taking action is a powerful tool in your action-mindset toolkit. Taking account of what really matters to you and asking yourself how going after it might make a difference in your life can clarify why *not* acting is a bad idea that will probably make you feel worse.

Next, you need an action plan of moves—even tiny ones—that you're prepared to make, and then you need to actually make them. Strengthening and sustaining new habits requires practicing these steps. Sometimes you're going to backslide, and that's normal and okay. Don't get discouraged!

CHAPTER 4

GET SET

Face Your Discomfort and

Map Out an Action Plan

In this chapter, we'll consider how one teen feeling stuck in avoidance works on overcoming his discomfort.

SAM'S family recently moved to a new town in the middle of fall semester. He misses his friends and really wishes he could make some new ones, but he's so nervous about striking up a conversation with kids at school that he's been skipping lunch every day to work on his homework in the media center. He avoids getting to his classes early and rushes out the second the bell rings, so it won't be obvious to everyone that he has nobody to hang out with. He knows that if he tries to talk to someone, he'll sound completely dumb!

The acute nervousness that Sam feels when he imagines interacting with other teens disappears temporarily when he steers clear of such situations. But the longer he avoids reaching out to other people, the lonelier and more down on himself he feels—and the more anxious about the next situation. It becomes tougher and tougher to venture into the cafeteria and find a seat in the crowd, and more and more appealing to spend all his free time in his room playing video games and streaming movies.

NO PAIN, NO GAIN!

How can Sam break this cycle and begin to make progress toward his goal of having friends? One certainty you can count on is that life is filled with uncertainty, so this is a skill we all need to call on every day. Learning to tolerate and even welcome discomfort is a normal and necessary part of growing up and taking on new responsibilities and challenges. It can help ease your resistance if you replace the big flashing "but" that's creating a barrier in your head with an "and." Instead of telling yourself that you'd really like to make a move, but it will be impossibly hard, think, *This step will be hard,* and *I'd really like to take it.*

It's true that having to accept the psychological pain that comes from facing and fighting distressing anxiety or depression might feel especially difficult. But think about it: You're probably already practicing this skill in some areas of your life.

For example, you may be willing to get up before dawn and run two miles every morning when you're training to improve your performance in the next cross-country meet. And you don't mind suffering through a couple of extra hours of study before a big test when bringing your C to a B will convince your parents to give you a later curfew. The discomfort you experience in both cases is worthwhile because it's helping you to accomplish goals that matter to you.

Well-known psychologist Robert Leahy describes the kind of discomfort that produces progress toward our goals as "constructive" discomfort. He points out that the price of *not* acting is also discomfort—in Sam's case, disappointment in himself and reinforced fears, not to mention continued loneliness. This, Leahy says, is "useless" discomfort (Leahy 2005).

Taking a moment to consider that perspective can sometimes give you the boost you need to get going. If you'll be uncomfortable either way, why not go after what you want?

ONE SMALL STEP AT A TIME

And remember, even tiny steps toward your goals are fine—the point is to start! In any challenging situation, breaking a task down into incremental steps can make it seem less challenging and more manageable. And when it's worry or anxiety that has you stuck, the chances are good that you'll develop confidence with each step, and that your discomfort will gradually ease as you face it down and take satisfaction in your progress.

In fact, psychologists rely on a small-step approach to help people of all ages overcome the worry and anxiety—even paralyzing phobias like a fear of flying or snakes—that are keeping them on the sidelines of life. Together, for example, a therapist and a person seeking help would plot out a series of actions, known as *exposures*, that give the person practice experiencing the discomfort each act produces. The first couple of steps are relatively easy, and then gradually the steps become more and more difficult as the person's comfort level adjusts and the realization hits: *This isn't as bad as I expected!* This approach, which we are calling a staircase exposure exercise, puts your goal on the top step.

The same principles can also help teens who are stuck because they feel sad or depressed. They avoid people or situations, and let their homework and other responsibilities slide, because they simply don't have the energy and will to act. Making yourself get off the couch and take part in an activity that you've enjoyed in the past, and continuing to schedule such outings into your calendar, can not only ease your discomfort with taking action but also surprise you by lifting your mood. Psychologists call this process *behavioral activation*: identifying pleasurable activities and doing them even when you don't want to.

You can try the exposure approach or behavioral activation yourself. (We'll talk more about behavioral activation in chapter 8.) Let's see how the exposure process might work for Sam.

A PATH TO THE CAFETERIA: SAM'S EXPOSURE PLAN

The social circle Sam enjoyed before his family's move had been tight since kindergarten, and he always had good friends around to hang out with during school, to play pick-up basketball with in the park after homework, and to make plans with on weekends. He misses that camaraderie so much that it's easy for him to identify his key value—close friendships—and his motivation for wanting to stop hiding out in his room. Would his life be a lot more fun next month if he figured out how to reach out and make some friends? *Yes!*

Sam realizes his main problem is that he's way out of practice meeting new people, and his self-talk is telling him that everyone will think he's boring and uncool. But when he stops to ponder whether the self-talk is accurate, he has to admit that his old friends never seemed to think he was boring (well, almost never!). They actually thought he was pretty hilarious and fun to be with. So he comes up with an exposure plan to help him get over his nervousness:

1. He starts by jotting down a few open-ended questions he can use as conversation starters and practices playing out a few dialogues in front of a mirror.

2. Next, he requires himself to strike up a conversation with two adults in the community—a relatively easy start, because he's most nervous and self-conscious around teens he'd

like to befriend. He starts with the guy taking orders at the pizza place. The second conversation is with a young dad down the street who often is out dribbling and shooting baskets in his driveway. As he was hoping, it results in an invitation to join in. As these people respond to Sam's overtures with friendly interest, he gets more comfortable speaking up.

3. Sam next zeroes in on a guy he'd like to get to know in his math class, Marco, who seems to be friendly and is also in the same Spanish class immediately following math. He catches up to Marco as they head for Spanish class, says hi, and asks a question about their latest reading assignment. Marco asks Sam where he used to live and where he lives now, and the conversation goes naturally from there. They start walking together between class regularly.

4. Because Sam really enjoys taking photos, he asks the yearbook adviser if he can join the staff even though it's pretty late in the semester. The idea of coming into the club after everyone has settled in and started working together is really daunting, but he realizes that the work will give him a natural way to connect with classmates who share his interest. Once he joins, he has work assignments to talk about.

5. As a way to calm his nerves, Sam takes a few deep breaths before he tackles his ultimate goal—heading to the cafeteria for lunch and some socializing. He hopes he'll spot Marco or someone from the yearbook staff to sit with, but he doesn't. He takes a spot at a table with several empty seats, where a couple of guys are disagreeing about a movie they just saw. After he nods hello and listens for a couple of minutes, Sam asks a question about the movie when the guys pause to take a bite. As the conversation continues, he notices Marco and one of his buddies walk by, and waves them over. Pretty soon all five are talking about movies.

As you can see, each new step forces Sam to face and adjust to a greater degree of discomfort. But with all the practice, and with each bit of progress along the way, his uncertainty and nervousness ease. He feels proud of the headway he's making in finding his place at school. And he's optimistic that he's on the way to establishing new friendships. You'll get the chance to create your own multistep plan at the end of this chapter, imagining it as a staircase with the easiest step at the bottom and the final one—arrival at your goal—at the top.

LEAN ON YOUR INTERESTS AND STRENGTHS

One strategy that helped Sam accept and experience discomfort is that he planned some of his actions based on activities he enjoys and is good at: basketball and photography. Do you love art or music or skateboarding? Can you think of ways to map your own action plan so that it builds upon your interests and strengths?

Another way to rely on your interests for support is to use them to reward yourself for each advance you make by buying something useful for a favorite activity, say, or by doing something you enjoy. Sam might tell himself that each conversation with a stranger allows him to spend an hour shooting baskets or editing his photos, for example. His first lunch in the cafeteria might be worth the new camera lens he's been saving for.

And if anxiety, sadness, or discouragement has been causing you to procrastinate, or to throw up your hands in defeat before even trying, a series of small rewards can often help you get started and then stay focused. Suppose you feel so anxious or gloomy about pulling off your section of a group history presentation that you've been avoiding doing any research. An effective reward system might be to treat yourself for buckling down by allowing fifteen minutes of skateboarding or video gaming or reading a good thriller after every forty-five minutes of work.

THE HANDY SKILL OF RELAXATION

If, as you prepare to take the plunge, your stomach is churning, and rapid breathing and a racing heart are making you dizzy, a quick relaxation exercise can come to the rescue. Close your eyes and slowly take a few deep breaths before you act, for example. Clench your muscles and then consciously relax them. And, as you walk toward a scary situation like Sam did on his way to lunch, restrict your focus to the current moment, to putting one foot in front of the other. Being mindful only of the present, rather than worrying about what will happen next, can ease your physical and emotional distress.

★ ★ ★ FOR YOU TO DO ★ ★ ★

The exercises that follow will help you see how it's possible to adjust to constructive discomforts that come with taking brave steps toward your goals. Part of the secret is learning to accept and sit with the uncomfortable feelings rather than fight them, and part is to understand your motives and come up with a well-designed multistep action plan. While it often helps to give yourself a reward for each successful step up your staircase of actions, you might find that your growing sense of pride and self-confidence is reward enough!

Practice Getting Comfortable with Discomfort

Your goal in this exercise is to practice accepting and tolerating the discomfort that has been holding you back from accomplishing something that is important to you. Describe a time when your discomfort—a fearful thought, say, or a negative emotion or distressing physical sensation—prevented you from taking action. Maybe you wanted to join a group of classmates or speak up in class or visit a new place, for example, but opted not to do so to avoid discomfort.

_____

_____

_____

_____

_____

_____

_____

Now close your eyes and visualize the situation in your mind, conjuring up all the types of discomfort you're aware of. Maybe you feel so anxious that your heart is racing or your stomach hurts or you're overwhelmed by a great sense of dread and fear. Jot down your emotions and body sensations, using a new row for each type of discomfort. In the next column, rate how uncomfortable you are with each feeling as it arises, with 10 being the most intense. Now, sit with each discomfort until you feel the intensity ease. Practice this visualization until you sense that you could manage your distress and take a step toward your goal. Rate your discomfort level again in the final column when you reach that point.

➡️ **Download a copy of the chart at http://www.newharbinger.com/50461.**

EMOTIONS AND BODY SENSATIONS	DISCOMFORT LEVEL AT THE START (0-10)	DISCOMFORT LEVEL AFTER VISUALIZATION (0-10)

What did you expect to happen when you started this exercise?

_____

_____

What did happen?

_____

_____

⭐ It's common for teens to discover that their expectations of how awful the discomfort would be are way, way off target!

Reward Yourself for Your Effort

To develop a habit of taking action—an action mindset—and break a pattern of withdrawing or avoiding, we need to repeat pushing through our discomfort over and over again until the practice sticks and acting becomes more automatic. After you learn how to ride a bike, you no longer have to keep thinking about pushing the pedal and braking. You just do it.

One effective tool when building a new habit is to reward yourself for each success. Let's develop a list of pleasant activities that would make you feel rewarded.

Ask yourself: *What do I find fun? What puts a real, true smile on my face?* Start by looking at the possibilities below. Circle any that might work for you. Or if you are feeling blah right now and not excited about much, what gave you some pleasure in the past?

Then add your own ideas on the lines below the list. Note any tangible gifts you might like to give yourself too. A small reward might be stickers or stars or smiley faces. Or maybe you've been saving for a video game or book.

★ **LISTEN TO MUSIC**	★ **SKATE**	★ **READ CARTOONS**
★ **PLAY MUSIC**	★ **SKI OR SNOWBOARD**	★ **PAINT**
★ **GO SHOPPING**	★ **SKATEBOARD**	★ **TAKE A BATH OR SHOWER**
★ **GO TO SPORTS EVENT**	★ **TRAVEL**	★ **SOAK IN A HOT TUB (IN YOUR IMAGINATION, IF THERE ISN'T ONE NEARBY)**
★ **WATCH A SPORTS EVENT ON TV WITH FRIENDS**	★ **GO ON VACATION**	
	★ **BAKE**	★ **SWIM**
★ **READ**	★ **DRAW**	★ **RIDE A BIKE OR SCOOTER**
★ **DO PUZZLES**		

★ WORK ON A HOBBY

★ RUN

★ WORK OUT

★ COOK

★ WRITE STORIES
  OR POEMS

★ DANCE

★ RELAX OUTDOORS

★ WALK IN NATURE

★ GO OUT WITH A FRIEND
  OR FRIENDS

★ PLAY VIDEO GAMES
  WITH FRIENDS

★ ORGANIZE

★ OTHER ACTIVITIES AND
  GIFTS YOU CAN GIVE
  YOURSELF:

★ _____

★ _____

★ _____

★ _____

★ _____

★ You can use your list to help make the hard work ahead more appealing. Be kind to yourself and enjoy some treats to celebrate your progress. Sometimes you might not have the time or money to give yourself a reward in the moment, but you can experience some of the pleasure by visualizing it in your mind.

Break Through the Barriers

This exercise will give you practice identifying when and why action is important, what discomforts you feel that are holding you back, and manageable steps you can take to break through those barriers. First, consider Armen's story and the process that leads him to action. Then try out this process yourself.

> **ARMEN** by his own description is an overachiever. He cares about his grades and performance, works really hard, and hates the idea of not doing well. However, he gets very uncomfortable when he's the center of attention and rarely speaks up in class. He worries that what he has to say cannot possibly be as smart as what his classmates would offer, and that he'll stumble over his words or forget the point he wants to make. At the same time, thinking about speaking up makes him physically shaky, and his stomach feels upset. This is a big problem for Armen, because participation in his history class counts for 25 percent of his grade. He badly wants to excel so he can get into a more advanced history class next semester.

How can Armen get from Get Ready! to Go!? He first identifies what is important to him and examines what is holding him back, then creates a staircase of increasingly challenging steps that will help him adjust to and tolerate his discomfort. Help him "Get Ready!" by filling in the blanks.

GET READY!   **VALUES.** What does Armen value that makes speaking up important?

_____

_____

MOTIVATION. A motivational question he asks himself is *How will my life be better if I learn to speak up in class?* His answer:

_____

_____

_____

DISCOMFORT. What self-talk is causing him to fear taking action? What bodily sensations?

_____

_____

_____

Armen plans a staircase of steps to ease himself into talking in class. He arranges the steps from easiest to hardest, with the easiest at the bottom. He can change them around as he goes, if needed. Some steps might take more tries than others.

Armen congratulates himself for the effort it took to climb his staircase.

ARMEN'S GOAL:

Initiate a comment during class discussion.

Raise my hand and answer one question in class.

Have my friend quiz me on a few history questions.

Watch (or listen to) myself answering a question at home.

Record (video or audio) myself answering a question at home.

Come up with a question from our assignment and practice answering it at home.

ARMEN STARTS HERE. Watch one of my classmates answer a question and notice how he sounds and how everyone reacts.

GO! Armen takes his first step the next day. As he climbs, he asks himself what he had expected would happen when he took action, and then what actually happened. His answers help him learn that expectations beforehand are often a lot worse than reality!

Try It Yourself

Use the space below to describe a situation from your own life in which, like Armen, you're avoiding action. Feel free to use the same situation you used in activity 10 if you like. Then work your way from Get Ready! to Go!

_____

_____

_____

_____

 **VALUES.** What do you value that makes change important? Look back at your list in chapter 3.

_____

_____

MOTIVATION. Look at the list of motivational interviewing questions in chapter 3 and answer two of them here.

_____

_____

_____

_____

DISCOMFORT. What self-talk is causing you to fear taking action? What bodily sensations?

 Make a plan and create your staircase below. Write down some actions you can take to slowly face your discomforts, and then put them in order from easiest to most difficult. You can change these as you climb the staircase, even adding a few steps as needed. Sometimes you can mount your stairs one after another, but sometimes you might need to go back a step or two and try again.

Congratulate yourself for the effort it took to climb your staircase.

 YOUR GOAL:

START HERE.

Download a blank staircase at http://www.newharbinger.com/50461.

Once you get to Go!, describe your first action and how it went. Think about what you expected to happen. What actually happened?

_____

_____

_____ hhhhhhhhhhhhhhhh

_____

Place yourself on your **READY!-SET!-GO! METER** when you feel ready to assess your progress. Remember: Don't worry if you need to backtrack on the way forward.

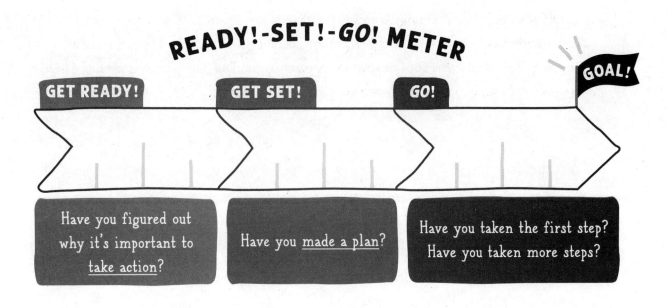

Congratulations! You're now on the move toward where you want to be.

 **KEY TAKEAWAYS**

REMEMBER THAT LEARNING TO TOLERATE (AND EVEN WELCOME) THE DISCOMFORT that comes with uncertainty is a normal and necessary part of stretching and growing. Practicing that skill is a key step in making progress toward your goals and becoming fully engaged in your life.

One effective way to gradually adjust to discomfort is to work your way up a staircase of small but increasingly challenging steps toward your goal. This series of actions, which psychologists call exposures, gives you practice experiencing—and tolerating—the discomfort each act produces. You realize: *This isn't as bad as I expected!*

You can use your personal strengths and interests to stay motivated to succeed. For example, it's smart to build an action plan around activities that you love and feel good at, so you're more confident as you get started. Likewise, rewarding yourself for each success with an activity that gives you pleasure can be a great way to keep yourself moving forward.

CHAPTER 5

WHEN YOU WORRY

How Action Can Help Quiet

Your Inner Voice of Doom

Many teens facing uncertainty immediately begin imagining all the worst-case possibilities that might unfold. This type of chronic worry, which is called *catastrophizing* or "what if...?" thinking because it involves habitually anticipating disaster, is a very common cause of anxiety in teens and adults alike. And not surprisingly, the automatic expectation of a bad outcome is a powerful force keeping teens from taking positive but risky steps toward their goals. People with a worry habit tend to avoid all kinds of challenges, from parties and meeting new people to learning to drive to situations that require speaking or performing in front of others.

Suppose, for instance, that your best friend has been less available than usual the past couple weeks since you both moved up to a large high school. Often, she doesn't respond to your texts for hours, which is unlike her. You're positive this means she's trying to drop you as a friend now that she's meeting much more interesting new people. You've been hoping to hang out with her at the football game after school, but the thought that she might ignore you and sit with other classmates hurts and is giving you stomach pains. So maybe you just won't go.

Or suppose you've been selected to make a class presentation on your group's science project. The report will count for 30 percent of your group's grade on the project, so everyone is counting on you to nail it. But you're convinced you're going to mess up and make a fool of yourself, sweating and stumbling as you forget what you want to say. You're especially worried that you'll be responsible for getting the group a low grade. Maybe you can email your notes to someone else and stay home sick that day.

IS FAULTY THINKING KEEPING YOU STUCK?

Worry about what's ahead isn't always problematic, of course. Often, the alarm we feel in an uncertain situation is right on target, and can be helpful or even keep us out of trouble. You'd be wise to be concerned about taking a test in two days, for example, if you haven't yet opened the book. But if you see yourself in either scenario above, it's important to understand that it might be your own unrealistic—and correctable—thinking that's causing you to suffer and avoid action. Your mind predicts that something awful is looming even when there's little or no reason to assume that the prediction will come true.

In the first case, for example, the only evidence you have that your friend is trying to avoid you is her delay in texting you back. Isn't it more likely that she's just busy and distracted by the new demands and excitement of starting high school?

And even if you're nervous about losing your train of thought in front of the class, why is it a given that you'll make a fool of yourself? Perhaps you can head off any possibility of that by creating a slide presentation and practicing in front of your family.

It's possible to examine the gloomy or panicky predictions getting in the way of positive action and recognize that they're most likely unreasonable—false alarms. Ask yourself what self-talk is freezing you in your tracks. (*She obviously doesn't want to be friends anymore!*) What evidence do you have of that? What's more likely to be true? (*She hasn't been very responsive these last few days, but high school is really busy. She's probably just overwhelmed.*)

Once you've developed a more realistic, on-target view of the situation, you'll feel much more comfortable about taking positive steps, even if they're tiny ones. (*I'll find her at the game and ask her how everything's going. If she's with other people, I can still say hi and be friendly.*)

THE ACTION-FIRST APPROACH

Sometimes pesky or panicky thoughts just feel too hard to tame. You might find that it pays off in a big way to take a deep breath, quiet the thoughts a bit, and decide to act anyway. That's because those CBT pillars—thoughts, actions, and feelings, both physical and emotional—are so interdependent that your actions affect your thoughts and the way you feel.

For example, you decide to just go to the football game and join the group your friend is with. Nothing terrible happens—in fact, you talk for twenty minutes with someone new. You realize that rather than lose your best friend, you'll probably be able to make new ones. A small success, or even simply your realization that your expectations were not accurate and disaster is *not* always the outcome, will help you feel calmer and more confident and less physically shaky or sick. And you'll become more optimistic about the future and your power to affect it. That will feel good!

GETTING COMFORTABLE WITH PHYSICAL DISCOMFORT

As we discussed and practiced in chapter 4, implementing your action plan involves accepting and adjusting to the discomfort that uncertainty brings. Many teens with a serious worry habit have to deal with a double whammy: the discomfort of not knowing how a situation will turn out plus the range of hard-to-bear physical sensations that anxiety often triggers.

The panicky racing heart and dizziness, for example. The dripping sweat, stomach cramps, and nausea that—horrors!—might cause you to vomit in public. Sometimes, in fact, a teen's worry about experiencing such bodily sensations is a greater barrier to action than worry about the specific challenge itself.

We've learned that it's possible to adjust to the mental discomfort associated with action by exposing yourself to increasing doses of it through small, progressively more difficult steps. In much the same way, teens whose anxiety triggers such physical discomforts can create similar sensations in their bodies—by spinning around in circles to generate dizziness and nausea, for instance—and practice experiencing them.

Therapists often use this technique, known as *interoceptive exposure*, to help anxious or panicky clients realize that it's possible to cope with these sensations. A therapist might guide a person to hyperventilate, for example, to experience the light-headedness and tingling sensations that often result. If you're petrified that your heart will race and you'll start dripping sweat in a social situation, you might run around the block on a sunny day to see what that would feel like. The idea is that you'll realize that you can tolerate this discomfort, and that it will pass.

★ ★ ★ FOR YOU TO DO ★ ★ ★

In the following pages, you'll get practice recognizing off-target worries and coming up with more realistic and helpful ways of thinking and responding. You'll also experiment with exposing yourself to physical discomforts as a way to lessen their power to keep you on the sidelines. Finally, we demonstrate the power of a mindfulness practice, which brings your focused attention to the present moment rather than the past or future, to calm both your mind and your body.

Manage Your Off-Target Worries

Teens who avoid action because they expect the worst to happen are very often basing their worry on unrealistic, off-target thinking. Pausing to give themselves a reality check and come up with a more on-target thought can be the boost they need to move forward. Read Ani's example, and then read each situation that follows and write down a more realistic, on-target way to see the situation. Next, come up with a proactive step that would be much more productive than avoiding action. Consider the benefits of acting, and note one consequence of deciding to stick to the sidelines instead.

ANI is working on a group project. She worries that her ideas will be ignored, so she's afraid to speak up.

- **MORE ON-TARGET THOUGHT:** Ani realizes there's no reason to think the group will ignore her ideas. Everyone is expected to contribute, so they'll probably be happy to get her suggestions.

- **PROACTIVE STEP:** She bounces her ideas off one of her friends first.

- **CONSEQUENCE OF NOT TAKING ACTION:** The group is likely to be upset with Ani if she sits back and lets them do all the work.

AUGUST is shy and worries about not fitting in with the teens in his theater class. He decides not to try out for a part in the class play.

- **MORE ON-TARGET THOUGHT:** _____

- **PROACTIVE STEP:** _____

- **CONSEQUENCE OF NOT TAKING ACTION:** _____

TAYLOR gets a queasy stomach the day she has to write an essay in history class and, though it hasn't happened before, she's worried that she might throw up at school. She's so afraid of being humiliated that she decides to stay home sick.

- MORE ON-TARGET THOUGHT: _____

- PROACTIVE STEP: _____

- CONSEQUENCE OF NOT TAKING ACTION: _____

HENRY feels really insecure about asking someone to go on a date. He's worried that he'll be rejected, so he decides to avoid the upcoming school dance.

- MORE ON-TARGET THOUGHT: _____

- PROACTIVE STEP: _____

- CONSEQUENCE OF NOT TAKING ACTION: _____

THEO is anxious and down because he doesn't have set plans for this weekend. He resigns himself to hanging out at home, doing nothing particularly interesting.

- MORE ON-TARGET THOUGHT: _____

- PROACTIVE STEP: _____

- CONSEQUENCE OF NOT TAKING ACTION: _____

Now think about one situation that has upset you and caused you to choose inaction.

DESCRIBE IT HERE.

_____

_____

_____

_____

_____

_____

● **MORE ON-TARGET THOUGHT:** _____

_____

● **PROACTIVE STEP:** _____

_____

● **CONSEQUENCE OF NOT TAKING ACTION:** _____

_____

⭐ What will you discover as you get better at recognizing your off-target thoughts? The more realistically you see situations and the more proactive plans you generate, the better your mood will be.

Tame Your Physical Sensations

Simulating the physical sensations we often feel when we are anxious, upset, or down helps us realize that what we think about these sensations is almost certainly not accurate. We might worry about dying or fainting when our heart races or we can't catch our breath, for example. We might fear that we'll throw up when our stomach starts churning, or that people will see us sweating. As we have learned, the fear of these physical discomforts often leads to avoiding situations and people that might trigger them. But we also know that if you purposely expose yourself to these bodily sensations, you learn that they typically diminish in intensity *and* that you can handle them.

Everyone has different feelings in their body as a result of anxiety or upset. Use the outline here to indicate the area of your body that is most affected and describe the sensations you experience when you feel anxious or upset. Note which bodily sensations are most distressing to you and prevent you from taking action.

You can bring on the bodily sensations that bother you in a controlled situation. Before you try the activities that follow, make sure you're in a place where you feel safe and know that you can stop at any time if you begin to feel overwhelmed. Notice how the physical sensations you bring on make you feel, and how they slowly fade away when you return to a normal, more relaxed state.

➡ **Download the outline at http://www.newharbinger.com/50461.**

- If breathlessness or a racing heart bothers you, run up and down stairs until you feel out of breath. Or jump in place for one to two minutes until you have that feeling.

- If you worry about feeling queasy or light-headed, bend at the waist and then bring your body up quickly a few times. Or shake your head from side to side for thirty seconds.

- If your stomach tightens when you get anxious, pull your stomach in tight as if someone punched you in the stomach, and hold it for thirty seconds.

- If sweating distresses you, run around the block on a hot day.

As soon as you experience the sensation or sensations you're afraid of, stop and notice how you feel.

How distressing are the sensations?

_____

_____

_____

_____

How long do they last? What do you notice about their intensity?

_____

_____

_____

_____

Which of these activities produce sensations most closely resembling your own?

_____

_____

_____

_____

_____

⭐ Practice these exercises until the scary, distressing feelings become manageable and less threatening. Realizing that you can cope with some physical discomfort will give you the confidence to move forward and take action.

Stay in the Moment

Mindfulness is a practice that helps you fully focus on and attend to the present moment without judging what's going on. This strategy especially helps teens who constantly worry that something bad will happen in the future and teens who feel sad and depressed when they get stuck thinking about what happened in the past. The goal is not to stop your thoughts; that just makes the thoughts stickier and harder to move past. The goal is to interrupt or calm the unhelpful worry or dwelling in the past by bringing your attention and awareness to the present moment. A mindfulness exercise can be meditative and simply center on your breathing, or it can be centered around an activity.

⬤ TRY A BREATHING MINDFULNESS EXERCISE:

Slowly breathe out as much air as you can, as if you are blowing bubbles or into a balloon. Notice your chest deflate as the air leaves your lungs. Now slowly inhale. Notice the feeling in your shoulders and your arms as well as your chest. Focus only on the sounds and smells you experience, moment by moment, as well as your bodily sensations. Do this sequence three times.

⬤ TRY AN ACTIVE MINDFULNESS EXERCISE:

Get a piece of wrapped chewing gum or soft candy. Hold it in your hand. Focus all your attention on noticing the colors of the wrapper. Move the food to your nose and take note of how it smells. Now open and remove the wrapping. What sounds does the wrapper make? Notice the colors inside the wrapper. What color and shape is the candy? Place it on your tongue. Don't chew yet! Take a moment to detect the flavor. Start to slowly chew, and notice as it changes shape and texture. No judgment—what is, is!

⭐ When you attend mindfully, or do any activity mindfully, you begin to appreciate your life as it happens rather than fret about the past or future.

KEY TAKEAWAYS

IF YOU TEND TO WORRY CONSTANTLY ABOUT DISASTER AHEAD, it can be helpful to ask yourself, *Is there any evidence to support the predictions my mind is making?* Very often, fear of the future is a result of negative thinking that is off-target or simply not true.

Teens who chronically worry often must cope with the unpleasant bodily sensations triggered by anxiety as well as the uncertainty about how a situation will turn out. Simulating these physical discomforts in a safe environment—by running in place to generate a racing heart and breathlessness, for example—can help you learn to tolerate them.

Sometimes, taking action bravely even when your thoughts and sensations are shouting *No!* can actually help you manage those thoughts and sensations. Even a small success can make you feel proud and gain confidence, and realize that your worry was overblown.

CHAPTER 6

PARALYZING PERFECTIONISM

How to Stop Setting
the Bar Too High

In this chapter, we'll zero in on one specific worry that causes many teens to shrink from new challenges and avoid opportunities for fun in life: the anxiety-producing certainty that they'll make a mistake or fail in their own eyes. These teens set such a high standard for themselves—perfection—that any performance or outcome that falls even a little short of that ideal is an unacceptable failure. A perfectionist might feel ashamed and down after earning a 90 on a math test, for example, because anything lower than 100 isn't "good enough."

Do you recognize yourself in any of the following scenarios?

A group of teens from the neighborhood are hanging out in your friend's backyard and decide to set up the volleyball net. You wish you felt brave enough to join the game, but your serve has always been so erratic in gym class that you're sure you'll fail to get the ball over the net every time it's your turn. Rather than risk feeling like a loser, you tell your friend you have to head home.

All your friends are looking for summer jobs, and you'd like to apply for a position shelving books at your local library. You have to write a letter describing your strengths and why you think you're a good fit for the job, and even after five rewrites you aren't happy with it. If you can't even write a great letter, you think, you're obviously not right for the job. You don't apply.

Your science teacher has encouraged you to enter your astronomy project in the upcoming science fair. You're excited and flattered, but you are scared at the thought of the competition and nervous about having enough time to prepare an A-plus presentation for the judges. Rather than risk messing up, you tell your teacher that you have a family conflict that day.

Not surprisingly, perfectionists often feel upset with themselves and discouraged, both for letting themselves down when they choose to avoid taking chances and for constantly not meeting their own expectations when they *do* try. Over time, these teens exhaust themselves with unsuccessful efforts to achieve the impossible, and they miss out on countless opportunities because of their fears. They lose confidence in their capabilities. And sometimes all these feelings lead to depression.

PURSUE EXCELLENCE INSTEAD (AND YOUR PASSIONS)!

The problem with demanding perfection of yourself is that you're bound to be disappointed again and again, because it's an unattainable goal. On the other hand, wanting to do your best at whatever really matters to you is an admirable, healthy quality. A desire for excellence can inspire you to practice, work hard to reach your goals, and improve your skills and abilities. Being human means that we're bound to make mistakes, and that's okay—what matters is that we learn from them. Bouncing back and continuing to try are normal and necessary steps along the path to success.

If you doubt that your missteps can ever lead to good things, consider some examples of great success in spite of imperfection:

- Basketball phenom Michael Jordan didn't make his high school varsity basketball team when he tried out at first, and had to play junior varsity instead (Anderson 2019). In a 1997 commercial made for Nike, he described the thousands of missed shots and the many lost games of his career as being key to his success. "I've failed over and over and over again in my life, and that is why I succeed," he said.

- Apple cofounder Steve Jobs once told a graduating class at Stanford University that being publicly fired from the company at age thirty was devastating but that he decided to continue doing what he loved—working on new ideas and technology. Within five years, he'd started two new companies: the super-successful animation company Pixar and a computer start-up that Apple ended up buying, which brought him back to lead Apple again. Being fired, he told the graduates, was "the best thing that could have ever happened to me" (Jobs 2005).

- It was a mistake that led Alexander Fleming, a scientist who was researching ways to treat bacterial infections, to discover the life-saving drug penicillin. One day, he discovered that one of his cultures had been accidentally contaminated, and that mold was growing on it. But the good news was that the mold was preventing the bacteria from growing! Fhleming was later awarded a Nobel Prize for his discovery (Nobel Prize n.d.).

GETTING UNSTUCK: EXAMINE YOUR THOUGHTS

So how can perfectionists overcome their fear of mistakes and failing? As we discussed in the last chapter on worry, it may be faulty negative thinking that is holding you back. If so, you can examine those unfriendly thoughts and consider what is more likely true.

Many teens with perfectionist tendencies, for example, fall into the habit of all-or-nothing thinking. This means that they see the world—and their performance—in terms of polar extremes. If an outcome isn't terrific, it's horrible. If it's not a total success, it's a complete failure. They ignore the many (and more likely!) gradations of possibilities between those extremes.

To break the all-or-nothing habit, you can explore that range of other possibilities short of "complete failure." Sure, you've missed a few volleyball serves in gym class, but so have most of your classmates. And you haven't missed all of them. Besides, you're pretty good at returning the ball during volleys. Rather than an imperfect serve being a sign that you're a loser, isn't it more likely that your miss is just one of many misses a team deals with in a typical game?

As far as the science project goes, making a presentation that has a few stumbles in it isn't the end of the world. A couple of slips of the tongue won't change the fact that the research itself is solid. And you have time to practice describing it beforehand. You can always pause and refer to your notes if necessary.

Another common thinking habit that many perfectionists share is the "I should" habit. Teens who see the world in terms of what "should" happen hold themselves to rigid standards of what's acceptable. And they feel guilty, frustrated, and discouraged when they let themselves down (*I should have gotten an A!* and *I should have made that goal!*).

If this sounds like you, it can pay off in a big way to practice being a more flexible thinker. Are your "should" thoughts reasonable? Sometimes they will be, of course—for example, *I should study for my big test tomorrow* or *I should remember to call Grandma on her birthday*. Often, though, your "shoulds" are just expressions of your own unrealistic standards. Examining the many other possible outcomes that would actually be okay (or even fine!) can help you become more accepting of your own occasional (and perfectly normal) goofs.

GETTING UNSTUCK: PRACTICE IMPERFECTION

Obviously, accepting their own imperfection requires perfectionists to tolerate some discomfort, so the action-first exposure approach can also be very helpful when you're frozen in your tracks by fear of failing.

Therapists who work with teen perfectionists often rely on exposure therapy, guiding teens to practice tolerating this discomfort by purposely exposing themselves to it. They fall short of their own standards or make blunders on purpose, for example. Do you get stuck on one paragraph in an essay you are writing because it's not exactly as you want it to be, so you stop trying and put the assignment off? Make yourself get the paragraph down even though it isn't perfect, and then write the next one and the next until you've finished. Are you avoiding the science fair because of worry about presenting it to the judges? Try answering a question in class with the wrong answer, and then correct yourself.

Experiencing imperfect outcomes and adjusting to their consequences—which may be nonexistent, and almost certainly will be much less severe than you imagine they'll be—can help you become more flexible and accepting of yourself. And more willing to take a chance when you aren't sure you'll succeed.

GIVE YOURSELF A BREAK

Finally, think about this: What would you say to friends who make a mistake and feel down or angry at themselves? Perfectionists are often much more forgiving of others' goofs than they are of their own, and would naturally offer encouragement and compassion to a friend who messes up. You can try an experiment and do the same for yourself. Next time the voice in your head is demanding perfection or judging your performance harshly, try remembering your strengths and achievements. And give yourself credit—and some empathy.

★ ★ ★ FOR YOU TO DO ★ ★ ★

Can you appreciate the difference between expecting perfection of yourself and striving to do your best? The exercises that follow will help you make that distinction, a key step in lowering impossible-to-meet standards to a reasonable level. You'll also gain a better idea of how to expose yourself to the discomfort that comes with stumbling by purposely making mistakes. Finally, you'll take a few minutes to give yourself a pat on the back.

Go for Excellence, Not Perfection

Let's consider the difference between striving for excellence—a good thing—and wanting to be perfect, an unrealistic approach to life that leads to chronic disappointment. Read the list of perfectionistic behaviors in the first column, and think about how you might translate each one into a more realistic effort to simply do your best. Finally, what's one purposely imperfect step you can take to get better at tolerating the discomfort of making mistakes? In the third column, enter an exposure that would help you practice imperfection. The first four examples will give you the idea.

PERFECTIONISTIC BEHAVIOR	GOAL: TRYING FOR EXCELLENCE	EXPOSURE EXERCISE
Quitting the baseball team you joined with your friends because you strike out sometimes	Realizing that everyone occasionally goofs up, and working harder on your hitting	During practice, you swing and miss on purpose a few times.
Not being able to begin writing any of your reports until all your notes are perfectly recopied	Writing based on notes that are organized and readable, but not recopied	You allow yourself to rewrite the notes once without correcting anything. Next time, no recopying!
Drawing a picture for art class but not turning it in because it's not good enough	Working hard on a picture for class and turning it in on time	You draw a picture with your nonpreferred hand and give it to a friend.
Not responding in a group text chain with friends because you make typos	Typing carefully to reduce the risk of typos, and joining the conversation	You initiate a text with a friend and make a few typos.

PERFECTIONISTIC BEHAVIOR	GOAL: TRYING FOR EXCELLENCE	EXPOSURE EXERCISE
Declining an invitation from your dance teacher to join the team because you are not amazingly good at all aspects of the dance		
Deciding not to join your local summer swim team because—despite improving a lot last summer—most of your times were not good enough		
Deciding not to take an AP or honors class because it's so much harder to get all As		
Never participating in class because the answer might be incorrect		
Skipping a challenging extra-credit report because you're afraid you won't get an A-plus on it		
Not contributing project ideas to your small group in history class because your ideas certainly won't be good enough		

In the next activity, let's apply this same kind of analysis to a perfectionistic behavior from your own life.

Practice Imperfection:
Create Your Own Action Plan

Has your insistence on always being perfect sometimes prevented you from doing something you'd like to do out of fear of making a mistake? Describe the situation in the lines below, and then work your way toward a plan that will help you move from Get Ready! to Go!

 Describe a situation in which you avoid taking action, even though you would like to act, out of concern that you'll fail to be perfect.

_____

_____

How is being a perfectionist getting in your way? What is your motivation to change?

_____

_____

Can you translate your requirement for perfection into a more realistic statement of wanting to do your best?

_____

_____

 Create your plan. Think of two mistakes you can make (on purpose) in this situation to expose yourself to the discomfort of being imperfect. These exposures can make you realize that imperfection is not the end of the world—in fact, it's fine!—and help you overcome your reluctance to risk any missteps.

_____

_____

Bravely practice making your mistakes. What did you expect to happen? What actually happened?

As you make your way through this activity, visualize your progress by positioning yourself on the **READY!-SET!-GO! METER**. It can be very encouraging to watch yourself move toward your goal.

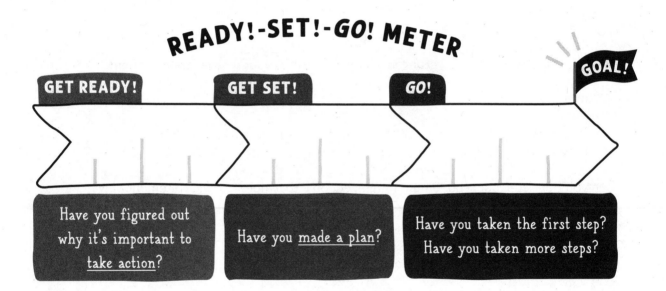

⭐ And it's worth repeating: Imperfection is not the end of the world—in fact, it's normal. In the next exercise, you'll get some practice putting your occasional stumbles into perspective by reminding yourself of all your wonderful strengths.

Try Some Self-Compassion

DAKOTA *gets really annoyed with himself when he makes mistakes or fails to measure up to his own high standards. The self-critic in his head makes him sad and frustrated, and he's in a perpetual state of disappointment that he hasn't done the right thing, or done enough. When his friends mess up, though, Dakota immediately shows them empathy and offers encouragement.*

Next time you notice that you're criticizing yourself for not being perfect, try pausing for a minute to give yourself some encouragement and credit for your many strengths.

When perfectionists practice being compassionate to themselves and appreciative of their good qualities and accomplishments, they can begin to view their flaws and missteps with greater acceptance and perspective. This can be freeing. It opens us to embracing and accepting our human "not-so-perfect" selves.

Describe an example of critical self-talk that has run through your head when you haven't met your own expectations.

_____

_____

_____

Now read the following sentences and fill in the blanks with examples of what you do well and your strengths as a person.

I WORK HARD AT _____

I AM CREATIVE! FOR EXAMPLE, I _____

MY FRIENDS LIKE THAT I _____

I AM A POSITIVE THINKER. FOR EXAMPLE, I _____

I AM HELPFUL WHEN _____

I HAVE A TALENT FOR BEING _____

MY BEST QUALITY AS A MEMBER OF MY FAMILY IS THAT I _____

I AM MOTIVATED TO _____

I AM BRAVE WHEN I _____

I AM _____

⭐ When you stop to remember you're actually pretty great, does it help you forgive yourself the occasional stumble?

KEY TAKEAWAYS

PERFECTION IS AN UNREALISTIC AND UNATTAINABLE GOAL. Striving to do your best, on the other hand, is a healthy approach to life that allows for missteps and failure. It's important to remember that trial and error are key components of learning and progress.

It might be faulty unrealistic thinking that's keeping you stuck. Many perfectionists with the all-or-nothing thinking habit see the world in polar extremes, for example, and ignore the wide spectrum of possibilities between success and total failure. Or they have the "I should" habit and set rigid rules for what's an acceptable outcome. You can challenge these thoughts by coming up with a list of the many other possibilities that would be just fine.

One good way to teach yourself to be more flexible is to practice being imperfect. You can gradually adjust to the discomfort that comes with making mistakes by purposely making a few. Then ask yourself, _What happened? Was it anywhere near as bad as I expected?_

CHAPTER 7

IS SOCIAL ANXIETY LIMITING YOUR HAPPINESS?

You Can Change That!

Remember Sam from chapter 4? As a new kid in school, he badly wanted to make friends, but he felt so nervous about talking to other students (he would sound stupid!) that he avoided eating lunch in the cafeteria. Sam's acute fear of social situations is so commonly shared by teens that it deserves a closer look in its own chapter.

Many people of all ages are shy, of course, and often need to give themselves a pep talk before they join a conversation or walk into a party or speak in front of a group. It's especially normal for teens, who are growing and changing so rapidly, to feel awkward and self-conscious and unsure of themselves in social situations where other people are observing them and might be forming opinions. There's nothing wrong with being shy.

But nervousness about how other people will react to you becomes a lot more problematic when it causes you to habitually avoid those conversations, skip the parties, and refuse to make a class presentation or audition for the school play even when you would like to participate. Yes, as we've noted before, avoidance may offer intense relief in the short run. But, long term, it only reinforces your sense that you can't handle discomfort and uncertainty. And it prevents you from developing relationships and from enjoying new adventures and opportunities. Most teens coping with social anxiety very much want to feel at ease with other people, so avoidance only interferes with their happiness. That's why developing an action mindset is so important.

Social anxiety manifests itself in many different types of situations, and some may cause you more distress than others. Like Sam, you might feel particularly paralyzed at the thought of joining other teens in conversation—of finding a seat in the cafeteria or going to a dance or birthday party and having to make small talk with classmates you don't know well. You might hate having all eyes focused on you as you answer questions in class, say, or perform your trumpet solo. Some teens are especially nervous about having to talk to teachers, doctors, and other authority figures; others dread having to compete on a team in gym class. And many socially anxious teens are terrified at the idea of dating or inviting someone to get together.

The discomfort of feeling uncertain about what will happen in these situations (and anticipating that it will be rejection and total embarrassment) is daunting enough on its own to keep many teens stuck in their rooms. But as we learned in chapter 5, the added fear of physical sensations that anxiety triggers can strengthen that inclination toward avoidance. Worry about a panicky racing heart, dry mouth, and stomach cramps can make it doubly difficult to imagine initiating a conversation or speaking up in class, for example. Do you automatically blush, stutter, or sweat when the spotlight falls on you? Getting up the nerve to engage with other people may require you to practice tolerating both types of distress.

EXAMINE YOUR SELF-TALK

Before we review how to practice tolerating discomfort, let's look at the distorted, off-target thinking patterns that can be a particular hurdle for socially anxious teens. Two common ones are the mind-reading habit and the fortune-telling habit.

Mind readers look at the other teens or adults in social situations they're in and automatically assume those people are thinking about them in a critical way. Suppose you see two teens from your neighborhood talking outside the grocery store as you approach, and you notice them glance your way at the same time that they start laughing. If you have the mind-reading habit, you're likely to think, *Wow, they're laughing at me. I guess they must not like me*, and head quickly into the store without saying hello.

Fortune tellers predict what's going to happen in a given situation—and it's unfailingly something bad. *When I get to the soccer game, no one is going to want to hang out with me*, you might tell yourself, and then decide not to go. Or *I'm not going to say what I think during our class discussion, because everyone will think my idea is dumb*.

When mind readers and fortune tellers immediately imagine a worst-case scenario, they're doing some catastrophizing too.

Remember, giving yourself a reality check and formulating more realistic self-talk (*Is there any evidence that they're laughing at me? Have they ever made fun of me or been unfriendly before? I bet one of them just cracked a joke.*) can often give you the confidence you need to take action. When you face your fear by taking small steps, and discover that your assumptions and predictions turn out to be unfounded, you gradually become more comfortable and self-assured. And you're likely to get the added boost that comes with success: satisfaction and a sense of pride for having taken a chance and joined the fun.

HOW TO GET COMFORTABLE WITH DISCOMFORT

If more realistic, friendly self-talk isn't powerful enough to get you moving, it may be time to also begin exposing yourself to the discomfort you've been avoiding. Many teens find that working their way up a staircase of increasingly challenging social interactions, as described in chapter 4, is very effective in helping them begin to tolerate both uncertainty about how events will unfold and feelings of self-consciousness and embarrassment.

Say, for example, that you've been wanting to join the concert band but are too scared to audition for a seat in front of everyone else who's trying out. The first (relatively easy) step on your staircase might be to practice the audition piece in your room in front of a mirror, imagining the experience of being on stage. Next, you might play the music for your family, and then gather two or three good friends for another performance. Finally, shortly before auditions, you could ask your music teacher or another trusted teacher to hear you play and offer some feedback.

Sam, you may remember, worked up the courage to join a group in the cafeteria by (1) practicing some conversation starters at home in front of the mirror, (2) starting conversations with two different adults in the community, and (3) catching up with another boy on the way to Spanish class and asking a question about the assignment.

Is dread of the uncomfortable physical sensations associated with anxiety (rapid heartbeat, shortness of breath, light-headedness, sweat) also an obstacle to action? You may benefit by practicing these sensations too. As chapter 5 discusses in more detail, it's possible to simulate such discomforts by jumping rope or running up and down stairs, for example.

Like most teens who get all this practice, you're likely to enjoy double benefits. Not only will your social skills improve as you climb your ladder, but you'll also realize that your fears about what would happen were overblown. Both these outcomes are confidence boosters, so your next social challenge should be less daunting. Sure, the situation might be a little awkward, and yes, you might have to work up your courage. But you can take small steps. You can cope.

★ ★ ★ FOR YOU TO DO ★ ★ ★

Now let's apply strategies you've practiced in previous chapters—challenging faulty negative thoughts and building a staircase of increasingly challenging exposures—to the fear (and avoidance) of social situations. Think about your motivations. Do you wish that you had more close friends and that you felt comfortable joining group activities? These techniques can be particularly effective when social anxiety is the issue.

Examine Your Thoughts

In this chapter, we learned about two off-target thinking habits common in socially anxious teens. If you feel anxious in social situations and/or when you are performing in front of others, it may be because you're telling yourself the outcome will be terrible (fortune-telling) or that others are thinking critically and negatively about what you said, how you looked, or what you did (mind reading). This exercise will help you challenge that negative voice in your head. First, read about Hunter's experience and answer the questions that follow.

As Hunter walked into a school basketball tryout with a friend, a few of the other guys looked up at him. He immediately thought, *They're surprised to see me here, because they know I'm not good enough to be on the team. They can tell I'm nervous and sweating, and they think I don't belong.*

LET'S HELP HUNTER EXAMINE HIS THOUGHTS.

What was Hunter's off-target thinking habit? What was his off-target thought?

_____

_____

_____

What do you think he is likely to do given these thoughts?

_____

_____

_____

How does he feel emotionally? Physically?

_____

_____

Reality check: What evidence does Hunter have that the other boys trying out are thinking he doesn't belong? What can he tell himself that's more realistic?

_____

_____

_____

What action can Hunter take based on his more realistic thought?

_____

_____

_____

NOW, DESCRIBE A SOCIAL SITUATION IN WHICH YOUR OWN MIND READING OR FORTUNE-TELLING CAUSED YOU TO FEEL VERY ANXIOUS OR TO AVOID THE SITUATION ALTOGETHER.

_____

_____

_____

_____

_____

What was your off-target thought?

_____

_____

How did it make you feel emotionally? Physically?

_____

_____

_____

Reality check: Was there any evidence supporting your thought? What could you have told yourself that would have been more realistic?

_____

_____

_____

If you find yourself in a similar situation again, what action could you take based on your more realistic way of thinking?

_____

_____

_____

Build Your Social Exposure Staircase

Remember, one very effective way to tackle a paralyzing fear of social situations is to make your way up a staircase of interactions (or exposures) that increase in difficulty as you progress upward. This small-step approach, which puts your ultimate goal on the top step, is designed to help you gradually adjust to your uncomfortable anxious feelings and gain confidence as you go. Let's observe how it worked for Chloe and then try it.

Now that Chloe is in high school, she worries that her mind will go blank when she tries to make conversation with someone new or with a group of her classmates. Her heart will race and her palms will feel sweaty. She thinks she'll look foolish and be embarrassed, so she limits her interactions to one friend from middle school, Jayden, and avoids any interactions with new people.

 Chloe realizes that this means she's missing out, and that Jayden is probably going to start making new friends and having fun without her. Plus, college is just a few years away, and she'll really want to have friends there.

 Chloe decides to create a staircase of increasingly challenging interactions that will move her toward her goal: getting comfortable befriending new people. The first step up is an action she thinks will be the easiest to try. That goal will be the final step at the top of her staircase.

 **CHLOE'S GOAL:**

Chloe congratulates herself for climbing her staircase.

Talk with two people I'd like to befriend but have been afraid to approach. Eventually, I will talk with them more than once!

Compliment someone new without Jayden.

Compliment someone at school when Jayden is with me.

Ask a classmate I know a question about our homework.

Go to the store and ask the cashier a question.

 Call and schedule a dental, hair, or medical appointment for myself or family member.

CHLOE STARTS HERE. Call and order a pizza for my family.

 GO! Chloe takes the first step. After completing each one, she asks herself if what she expected would happen actually did happen. When we become aware of how reality compares with our expectations, we often find that our fears were exaggerated. Of course, sometimes we find that a step is harder than expected, and we need to go back and insert an additional easier step. That's normal.

Next, try creating your own staircase.

Describe a situation in which your anxiety keeps you from engaging in social interactions or performing in front of other people.

_____

_____

_____

_____

What is your motivation for creating an exposure staircase and climbing it?

_____

_____

_____

On the next page, it's time to build your staircase. Start with the hardest step—your goal—at the top. Then, beginning at the bottom, list a series of increasingly difficult actions you can take to get there. You might need to repeat an action a few times before you're comfortable moving up to the next step, or you might need to go backward and add a step.

Congratulate yourself
for the effort it took to
climb your staircase.

START HERE.

 Begin climbing. Remember to ask yourself after each step whether your expectations before you started matched what actually happened. It can be empowering to see that you managed just fine, and that nobody judged you critically or found you foolish.

When you feel ready, use your **READY!-SET!-GO! METER** to visualize where you stand in your journey by shading in the bar or putting a mark at the point along the meter, for example. Remember, backsliding and trying again are normal, essential parts of making headway. You might replot your position several times in the weeks ahead, taking a step or two backward now and then in the process of moving forward.

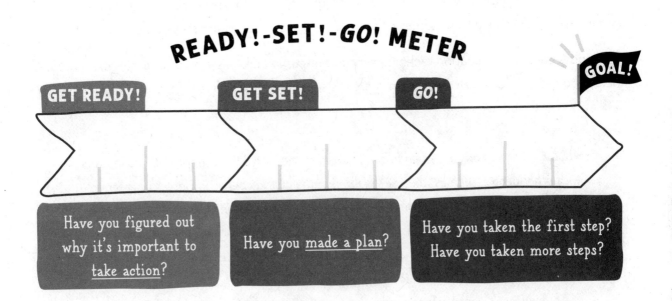

READY!-SET!-GO! METER

GET READY!   GET SET!   GO!   GOAL!

Have you figured out why it's important to take action?

Have you made a plan?

Have you taken the first step? Have you taken more steps?

Use Your Imagination

In one of the activities in chapter 4, you closed your eyes and imagined uncomfortable situations and feelings you've experienced, holding them in your mind until your discomfort eased. In a similar way, when you're having a great deal of trouble mustering the courage to engage with other people, it can help to first imagine yourself taking the necessary steps before you act.

Therapists call this visualization technique *imaginal exposure*. Like a staircase of actual exposures, it helps you get comfortable with discomfort. Let's see how it works, and then try it out.

ALEX feels very anxious when he's in a crowd or may have to acknowledge and interact with other people, such as when he's walking in the hallway between classes or entering a crowded room. He worries about what the other people are thinking about him, and his breathing and heart rate feel uncomfortably rapid. He typically keeps his head down and walks quickly to avoid any possible eye contact. His friends have asked him why he seems so unfriendly and doesn't ever say hi when they see him in the hall.

Alex doesn't want his friends and classmates to think he is unfriendly or stuck-up. And he really wants to feel relaxed in a crowd of people. But the thought of changing his behavior is so daunting that he decides to first practice being in a crowd in his mind, imagining himself handling progressively more difficult situations. This gives him an opportunity to gain confidence.

He starts by visualizing himself walking in the hall when most students are in class. He imagines himself walking with his head up and shoulders back. He paces his breathing.

Little by little, he adds more people to the image in his mind as he continues to keep his head up. He considers his worried thoughts about what people might be thinking and substitutes a thought like I'm a friendly person, and people feel good when others are friendly to them. Finally, he sees himself catching the eye of someone he doesn't know well. He imagines smiling and nodding and getting a smile in return.

Alex will likely still feel nervous the first time he translates his vision into reality. But watching the scenes play out ahead of time has prepared him to give it his best shot.

Now you try it.

Describe a social situation that makes you anxious and that you avoid. If you like, you can simply use the same situation you described in activity 21.

_____

_____

_____

_____

What thought typically runs through your mind that makes you feel anxious and want to avoid acting?

_____

_____

_____

_____

_____

⭐ Now take a few quiet minutes without distractions to close your eyes and imagine yourself in the setting alone. Gradually add the elements of the experience that make you fearful and see yourself handling them. Come up with a more realistic, encouraging thought. If you're afraid of entering a party, for example, you might slowly add more people to the room, then visualize yourself asking one person a question, then joining a group conversation. If making a presentation in class is what scares you, try seeing yourself at the podium with no one in the classroom, then imagine making your speech to a gradually growing group.

KEY TAKEAWAYS

THERE'S NOTHING WRONG WITH BEING SHY. But a problem arises when anxiety about interacting with other people causes you to avoid social situations. While avoidance may provide relief in the short run, it tends to reinforce in your own mind that you can't handle social situations.

Your unrealistic thoughts might be tripping you up. Many teens tend to be mind readers (who assume other teens in social situations are thinking about them critically) or fortune tellers (who predict that the outcome of participating in an activity will be bad).

Working your way toward a goal by exposing yourself to increasingly challenging social interactions is likely to provide double benefits: improved social skills and the reassuring realization that your fears about what would happen were misplaced.

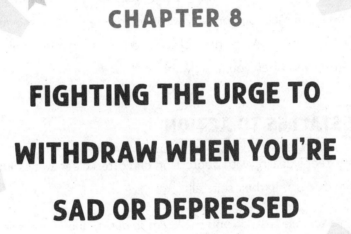

CHAPTER 8

FIGHTING THE URGE TO WITHDRAW WHEN YOU'RE SAD OR DEPRESSED

So far, we've focused on how fear and worry can hold you back in life, preventing you from taking on new challenges and seizing opportunities for fun. It's also true that many teens withdraw and hide out because they're overwhelmed by sadness or depression and just want to be left alone. It's very common when you are feeling sad to lack the energy or will to interact with other people and to see every activity as dull and pointless. In this chapter, we'll explore how faulty thinking may predispose you to depression and contribute to keeping you on the sidelines. We'll also look at how a strategy called *behavioral activation* can jolt you back onto your feet and help you begin to enjoy life again.

Basically, behavioral activation asks you to think about your values and interests and come up with activities based on them that you normally would enjoy—going to a movie or baseball game, hiking or swimming with a friend, taking an art class. Then you plug them into your schedule—and make yourself do them—even when you don't want to.

CHECK FOR OBSTACLES TO ACTION

As is true with anxiety, teens dealing with depression can often clear away some barriers to taking action by examining and adjusting their self-talk.

When you get a C on a science test, do you think, *I'm so dumb!* and *I'm terrible at science!*? Or when you miss a shot in a soccer game, do you tell yourself, *I'm such a loser!* and *I don't belong on the team!*? If so, you're engaging in a pessimistic style of thinking that psychologist Martin Seligman (1995) observed is common in people who are depressed. You tend to see your upsetting reality as being lasting rather than temporary, and as applying to your life in general rather than just to a specific set of circumstances: *I'm dumb!* as opposed to *I needed to study the concepts on this test more thoroughly; I'm a loser!* rather than *I was a little tired for today's game.*

You also tend to view such disappointments as evidence of your own personal weakness, and never as a result of other factors, such as *Wow, that was an unusually tough test!* and *The other team's defense was amazing!*

It's not surprising that teens who think pessimistically often feel hopeless about their future and helpless to have an impact on it—both key obstacles to believing in the power of an action mindset. It's also common to react angrily or irritably when you see yourself as a powerless victim: *Why even bother trying to make a difference in my life?*

Seligman also noticed that people who tend not to experience depression have a more optimistic, realistic thinking style. They view their disappointments as temporary, onetime setbacks—and even welcome them as learning opportunities. They also can recognize that a combination of factors may be responsible, rather than berating themselves for being personally to blame. There's plenty of room to feel hopeful about what comes next when you see the world this way.

And you *can* start to see the world this way! It's possible to develop a more optimistic thinking style by reminding yourself when something upsetting happens that disappointing situations and setbacks are temporary. They also are not a broad reflection of your capabilities and worth as a person. *Yes, this was tough, but it will pass. And I can do better next time!*

ZOOMING IN ON THE NEGATIVE AND OTHER DISTORTED THINKING HABITS YOU CAN BREAK

Dan has had a busy day. He got up early and went on a long run with two of his basketball teammates, followed by pancakes with them before school. His second-period math test seemed to go pretty well, and he got a B—whew!—on his English paper. During lunch period, his mom picked him up for a dentist appointment, which was pretty unpleasant but meant that he got to miss history class. Then, during basketball practice, Coach Harris told him he'd be starting in the next game.

Tonight, though, Dan is sprawled on his bed feeling totally bummed. When he said hello to a group of girls he knows who were leaving school at the same time he was, they kept talking and laughing and didn't respond. *It was so embarrassing!* he thinks. *What an awful day this was!* Dan has a hard time falling asleep because he can't get the painful moment off his mind, and he decides to avoid the girls if he sees them the next day.

Dan has an off-target negative thinking habit that many teens who are prone to sadness and hopelessness share: No matter how many "terrific" and "good" and "just okay" experiences they have in a day, their attention automatically zooms in on anything disappointing or hurtful, and they relive that experience over and over. The bad gets blown out of proportion in their mind, minimizing and even erasing all the day's pleasures and satisfactions. Deep in gloom, they see no reason to look forward to what comes next.

Other negative thinking habits that often lead to hopelessness—and inaction—include the "I can't" habit, the "I should" habit, and the self-blame habit. Do you think *I can't* when you're faced with trying something new or a little scary? You may constantly find excuses not to try and gradually lose faith in your capabilities. As you may remember from chapter 6 on perfectionism, "I should" thinkers have strict—and often unreasonable—ideas about how they ought to act and be: *I should get all As! I should be funnier!* When they fail to measure up, they get down on themselves and discouraged. "I should" thinkers sometimes have the self-blame habit, too—they hold themselves responsible for whatever goes wrong.

Do any of these thinking patterns sound familiar? If so, remember that you can break these habits by following these steps:

1. **EXAMINING THE EVIDENCE FOR YOUR ASSUMPTIONS.** For example, Dan can zoom back out for a look at the big picture and ask himself, *Was it really such an awful day? What went well? What fun did I have? What can I be proud of?* Teens who believe they can't possibly make a presentation in class might pause and recall the earlier times they've raised their hand and contributed a smart idea to group discussions.

2. **COMING UP WITH A MORE REALISTIC THOUGHT.** Once he puts his disappointment into perspective, Dan might realize, *I was bummed that the girls ignored me, but they were busy talking and maybe they just didn't notice.* The "I can't" thinker might say, *I may not have made a speech before, but I'm fine with speaking up in small groups. I can try!*

3. **FORMULATING AN ACTION PLAN.** Dan might choose to give the girls the benefit of the doubt and continue being friendly when he sees them. A teen facing a class presentation might think, *I'll get the hang of it ahead of time by practicing in front of my friends.*

MAKE A SCHEDULE—AND STICK TO IT

Sometimes it's beneficial to go straight to the action plan, and let your efforts and successes generate more hopeful, realistic thoughts. This is the theory behind behavioral activation, a technique developed and refined by multiple researchers, primarily Peter Lewinsohn, Neil Jacobson, Sona Dimidjian, Christopher Martell, and Carl Lejuez. Psychologists often use behavioral activation to help adults and teens who are so weighed down by unhappiness that they lack any will to act. It relies on key benefits of taking action that we've discussed before:

✓ When you take a step rather than avoid a situation, accepting that you'll feel some discomfort, you begin to master the discomfort. Avoidance often just makes the discomfort loom larger next time.

✓ Just going through the motions can improve your mood. In anxious teens, even small successes build confidence and provide a glow of satisfaction. When you're feeling down, making yourself go on that hike or join an art class can remind you of what matters to you and of the pleasure you've felt in the past.

To try behavioral activation yourself, start by reviewing the list of values you identified as important to you in chapter 3. Next, brainstorm a list of actions you can plug in to your daily planner over the next week that reflect those values and your interests. (For ideas, you may want to refer to the activities you identified in chapter 3 as good rewards for taking steps.)

If time spent reading and out in nature is important to you, for example, possibilities might include visits to the library and local bookstore and a hike and bike ride with a friend. You'll want to include one or two activities in your plan for each day, and spend a few minutes afterward assessing how each one has affected your mood. You may not see a change immediately, but keep at it.

Need a tug or a push to get out the door? Make a point of inviting friends or family members to join you on your outings. The moral support of someone who cares about you can make the difference when you're tempted to pull out of a plan and stay home. And having some company can enhance your fun.

★ ★ ★ FOR YOU TO DO ★ ★ ★

Your first task in the pages that follow is to practice spotting common thought distortions that lead to depression and then come up with more realistic, optimistic ways of framing the situation. Next, we'll help you identify a team of people you can turn to for support, which may help you fight the urge to isolate yourself from friends and family. Finally, you'll get a chance to try out behavioral activation, by committing to a week of activities that reflect your values and interests. Ideally, what you'll discover is that even going through the motions will remind you of past moments of enjoyment and lift your mood.

Recognize Distorted Thinking

As we've described in this chapter—and in more detail in *Conquer Negative Thinking for Teens* (Alvord and McGrath 2017)—your thoughts are extremely powerful even though they often are not accurate. This exercise will give you practice recognizing four common thinking habits that often lead to sadness and depression.

Read each statement and note which of the following thinking patterns it most closely reflects: zooming in on the negative, "I can't," "I should," or self-blame. Then come up with an alternative thought that's more hopeful and realistic.

THOUGHT: I'm not good at sports, so I won't sign up for soccer.

THOUGHT HABIT: _____

REALISTIC THOUGHT: _____

_____

_____

THOUGHT: It's so easy for Sahar to write an essay! It ought to be easy for me too.

THOUGHT HABIT: _____

REALISTIC THOUGHT: _____

_____

_____

THOUGHT: Angie isn't answering my texts. I'm a bad friend—I must have upset her somehow.

THOUGHT HABIT: _____

REALISTIC THOUGHT: _____

_____

_____

THOUGHT: Today was really awful! I got called on in English class and didn't know the answer.

THOUGHT HABIT: _____

REALISTIC THOUGHT: _____

_____

_____

THOUGHT: I'm not doing this homework. It's too hard.

THOUGHT HABIT: _____

REALISTIC THOUGHT: _____

_____

_____

THOUGHT: Why am I so shy? I ought to be able to go talk with them!

THOUGHT HABIT: _____

REALISTIC THOUGHT: _____

_____

_____

THOUGHT: Goofing up my lines at play practice ruined my whole day.

THOUGHT HABIT: _____

REALISTIC THOUGHT: _____

_____

_____

THOUGHT: I feel so dumb for striking out in the ballgame. It's all my fault that we lost.

THOUGHT HABIT: _____

REALISTIC THOUGHT: _____

_____

_____

⭐ As you shift your perspective by challenging those negative thoughts and coming up with a more realistic way of looking at the situation, you gradually become more hopeful and optimistic.

Build a Support Team

It's common when you're feeling down or depressed to withdraw from other people and believe you're all alone in the world. But you're *not* alone. Who are the people who care about you and stand ready to connect and help? Being able to ask for support or to bounce ideas off friends and family is crucial to gaining perspective about your life and difficult situations. And having a friend along on the outings that you're going to plan in activity 25 will help boost your self-confidence and your courage to get out there and have fun!

List as many sources of support in your life as you can think of. Consider trusted adults in your family and extended family and community: teachers, coaches, and family friends, for example. Add friends and siblings—perhaps even your pet. This is the team you will draw on when you need a friendly, supportive ear—or some company. You may want to download your list to your phone for easy access. Revisit your list every so often as you cultivate new relationships.

⬤ _____

⬤ _____

⬤ _____

⬤ _____

⬤ _____

⬤ _____

⬤ _____

⭐ It can be extremely hard to reach out to people when you feel sad, but doing so can be the key to getting yourself off the couch and out of the house. Furthermore, taking the initiative this way can shift your feelings of being helpless and hopeless to a sense of being proactive and more hopeful about the future.

➡ Download a support team list at http://www.newharbinger.com/50461.

Plot Out Your Behavioral Activation Plan

GET READY! In the first part of this exercise, you'll monitor your activities for the next week to see how you're spending your time now, and with whom. Note all your activities, including meals. Circle any that you did with someone else.

	MORNING	AFTERNOON	EVENING
MONDAY			
TUESDAY			
WEDNESDAY			
THURSDAY			
FRIDAY			
SATURDAY			
SUNDAY			

 Download blank planners at http://www.newharbinger.com/50461.

Next, take a look at the exercises you completed in chapter 3 that identified your values and your motives for getting outside of your comfort zone. Reviewing your values can help you take action, especially when it leads to an activity you enjoyed in the past when you were not so down.

 GET SET! Now let's draw up a one-week action plan in the planner that follows. You may want to refer to activity 11 in chapter 4 for ideas of what to schedule in. For at least a few of the outings, jot down a person from your support team that you'll invite along.

The idea is to create a schedule of activites that are rewarding, pleasurable, fun, gratifying, or even just okay. Examples might be playing music, going to a movie or sporting event with a friend, or going on a hike. Circle any that you do with someone else. Including a companion increases the odds that you'll follow through.

GO! Do at least one of your planned activities each day. Before you go to bed each night, make a note in the column on the right about how your actions affected your mood.

You can use the **READY!-SET!-GO! METER** to keep track of your progress whenever you feel ready to take stock. It can be especially tough when you feel depressed to move ahead in a straight line, and it's important to know that falling back a step or two is completely normal and to be expected. You can revisit your position on the meter—reconsidering the questions beneath the bar—as you continue to make an effort.

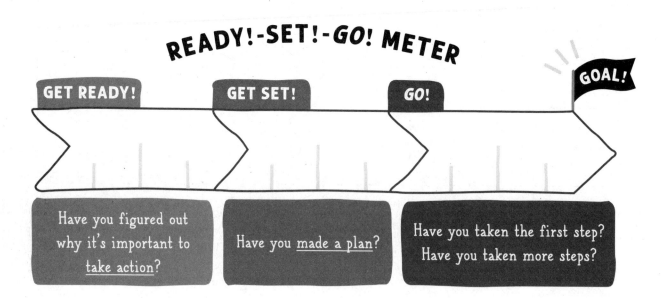

	MORNING	AFTERNOON	EVENING
MONDAY			
TUESDAY			
WEDNESDAY			
THURSDAY			
FRIDAY			
SATURDAY			
SUNDAY			

KEY TAKEAWAYS

DEPRESSION IS A COMMON REASON WHY TEENS WITHDRAW from other people and shy away from getting out and engaging in their lives. In their sadness, they often feel hopeless about the future and helpless to have an impact on it.

You can become more hopeful about your life (and more willing to participate in it) by paying attention to your thoughts, recognizing when they distort reality by being overly negative, and then coming up with more realistic thoughts.

Behavioral activation can help you fight the urge to withdraw and hide out. Psychologists have found that scheduling and taking action even when you don't want to, particularly when you include a friend, can lift your spirits by reminding you of past rewarding experiences.

CHAPTER 9

UNDERSTANDING THE DIFFERENCE BETWEEN ACTION AND HARMFUL REACTION

As we've seen, cultivating an action mindset—getting up the courage to meet new challenges as they arise, to seize opportunities, and to move purposefully toward your goals—can have a powerful effect on your sense of your capabilities and on your happiness.

Now let's consider for a minute why—and when—taking action can be counterproductive, a step that does more harm than good.

Remember, your thoughts, feelings, and behaviors are all interdependent, and that means your moods, as well as your thoughts, have a powerful effect on the way you act, just as the way you act affects your mood and how you think. (The message of this book in a nutshell!) For example, anger, irritation, and disappointment, common in people who are depressed, frequently cause them to act impulsively in a destructive way, lashing out at others or stalking off to sulk in their rooms. There's also a danger that such feelings can cause teens to strike out in frustration or disgust at themselves, perhaps by experimenting with alcohol or drugs, by skipping school, or by cutting themselves, for example.

Even in teens who are not depressed, feelings of annoyance and frustration are a common outcome of behaving passively—of just sitting back to see what happens in a challenging situation rather than proactively working to *make* something happen. If you end up being upset about whatever happened, there's a good chance you'll react by erupting in anger or irritation or sarcasm.

Not surprisingly, such negative reactions often create tension and hostility between friends and family members and, when directed at yourself, they can take a major toll on your self-esteem. Understanding the difference between productive, helpful action and harmful reaction can help you stop yourself from behaving rashly before you do harm.

It's worth noting that feelings of anger are often justified, of course. Sometimes, when you see an injustice or someone you care about has been badly treated, say, it's appropriate to feel angry. But even when that's the case, a thoughtful, productive response is bound to serve you much better than an angry outburst. You can assertively and calmly express your feelings, explain why you feel the way you feel, and suggest a way to rectify the situation. Rather than a lost friendship, the result might be an apology, a better understanding, and a satisfying solution to a problem.

HOW THINKING ERRORS CAN LEAD TO HARMFUL REACTIONS

Sometimes it's a distorted thought that triggers a destructive reaction. We've discussed before the way that "I should" thinkers beat themselves up when they fail to meet their own often-unreasonable expectations. In a similar way, teens with the "you should" habit get frustrated with or angry at friends and family members when they don't behave in the expected—"right"—way. If you have either or both of these thinking habits, you may know that it's not uncommon to react impulsively, sometimes doing harm to yourself or your relationships.

Other common thinking habits that can lead teens astray are the all-or-nothing habit, the "It's not fair!" habit, and the blame habit. You may recall from our discussion of perfectionism in chapter 6 that all-or-nothing thinkers see the world in polar extremes. When their unreasonably high expectations of themselves or of the way others should act are not met, they see the result as total failure. Similarly, when you see the world in terms of what's fair and what's not, you're apt to feel angry, frustrated, and victimized when people don't behave (and events don't unfold) the way you want them to. Expecting fairness is a recipe for disappointment because life simply doesn't work that way.

And if you have the blame habit, you may lash out in anger and hostility toward others when you consider your disappointments to be their fault. Or you may turn your anger and hostility inward if you tend to blame yourself for whatever goes wrong.

PREVENTING TROUBLE

If one of the problematic thinking habits sounds like you, remember: You can prevent trouble by catching yourself in an unreasonable thought—*It's not fair that she didn't invite me to her party!* or *It's all my fault that we lost the game!*—and asking yourself, *Is that really accurate? What's a more realistic way of looking at the situation?*

This kind of pause is often just what's needed to keep you from lashing out and to inspire a positive action instead. For example, you might think, *I know she couldn't invite everyone. Maybe if I suggest that we do something together after school one day, she'll think of me next time.* Or *It's too bad that I struck out in the ninth inning, but none of us played all that well today. We can do better with more practice.*

Whatever the reason behind that surge of irritation or hostility you're experiencing, pausing to take a few calming deep breaths or practice a brief mindfulness exercise (see chapter 5, activity 16) can be a powerful preventive step.

Pausing to calm yourself can provide the space you need to view the situation more reasonably and brainstorm a productive response that will improve rather than worsen it. When a friend makes you furious by rejecting your ideas for a class project, you can say, *You're being stupid!*—or you can take a breath and explain your thinking or suggest a compromise. If your plans to go to the beach with friends are threatened because your brother has a sudden conflict and can no longer drive you, you can berate yourself for disappointing your friends and go off on your own in frustration—or you can send out a group text asking for help finding another driver.

★ ★ ★ FOR YOU TO DO ★ ★ ★

Now, let's get some practice analyzing situations handled in an unproductive, harmful way and rethinking that response. When you're able to catch yourself before acting or reacting impulsively in anger, you may discover that you can find a way to improve matters rather than make them worse. In activity 27, we'll try out progressive muscle relaxation (PMR), another helpful method of taking that moment to calm down and think before making your move.

Turn Harmful Reactions into Healthy, Helpful Actions

Managing difficult emotions so that you act in a productive way—rather than reacting destructively and harming your relationships or your health—is an important habit to acquire as you become more independent and form new relationships. It involves aligning your actions with your values, and it's not easy. It takes practice.

The statements below depict some common scenarios in which strong emotions cause teens to react in a damaging way, counter to their own self-interest. Read Taylor's example, and then after each scenario, write an example describing how the teen might have handled the situation differently and more productively after pausing for a moment to calm down.

HARMFUL REACTION: After getting a bad grade on a test, Taylor skipped the rest of her classes that day because she was bummed and angry at herself and didn't want to face anyone.

HEALTHY, HELPFUL REACTION: Taylor went into the bathroom to take a few deep breaths and splash some cool water on her face as a way to calm down. After school, she emailed her teacher to ask if they could meet to review the questions she had missed on the test.

- *Dakota strongly disagreed with her friend Casey about their plans for the weekend. She started yelling at Casey, accusing her of being selfish.*

_____

_____

- *Angie was worried that Rory wouldn't understand why she wanted to hang out with a new friend, so she lied about what she was doing.*

_____

_____

● *Nathaniel confided in Blake that he was upset about being left out of the movie get-together the other night. When Blake didn't seem sympathetic, Nathaniel got angry and accused him of not being a good friend. Then he turned his back and walked away.*

_____

_____

● *Brady texted Rebecca to say that he couldn't get together as they had planned. Rebecca replied with a nasty comment.*

_____

_____

● *Steven got so angry when his brother backed out of driving him and his friends to the mall that he lost it and hit him.*

_____

_____

● *Jessie was really down on herself for avoiding her friends and not turning in her schoolwork. She felt alone and overwhelmed, and she cut herself.*

_____

_____

● *When the music director picked Jason to play a drum solo in the school concert, Logan was so upset that he skipped band practice the next two days and played video games instead.*

_____

_____

We hope that this exercise demonstrated the power of the pause! Now let's get comfortable and test one tried-and-true approach to relieving the pent-up tension that can cause you to strike out.

Calm Down with Progressive Muscle Relaxation

Progressive muscle relaxation is a strategy that helps you calm down by tensing and then relaxing your muscle groups one by one. Practicing this technique will help you become aware of how your body feels when you are at risk of reacting in a harmful way. Intentionally relaxing your muscles trains you to pause and release tension so that you are more likely to take a productive action instead. The more you practice, the easier it will be to recognize the tension buildup in time to cool off.

This practice has four parts. First, tense one muscle group at a time as tightly as you can and hold. Second, release the tension and relax the muscles. Third, notice the difference in the way the muscles feel when they are tight and tense and when they are loose and relaxed. Finally, scan your entire body to be aware of any muscles that might still be tense. After you relax, you might notice a cool or warm sensation or a tingling. Just be aware of the different sensations you experience.

TO BEGIN, GET INTO A COMFORTABLE POSITION AND CLOSE YOUR EYES. You are going to start at the top of your head and progress down to your toes. Raise your eyebrows and tighten your forehead. Hold that position. Hold it. Slowly bring your eyebrows to their resting position and notice as your forehead relaxes.

Now frown and squeeze your eyebrows together. Hold it tight. Hold it. Now, slowly let go and let those muscles loosen.

Move your way slowly down your face to your neck and shoulders, tensing up for a few moments and relaxing, noticing the difference in how your muscles feel when they are tense and when they are loose and flexible. From your shoulders, move slowly to your chest, your right and left arms and hands, your abdomen, your right leg, left leg, right toes, and left toes.

When you've finished, scan your body again to see whether any muscles still feel tight. Once your body feels completely calm and relaxed, slowly open your eyes.

Listen to a guided progressive muscle relaxation exercise at http://www.newharbinger.com/50461.

Write Your Narrative

As if you were writing an entry in your journal, describe a situation in which you reacted in a harmful way that you now regret. Perhaps you reacted harshly or abruptly toward someone else or with anger or disgust toward yourself. What thoughts, emotions, or body signals caused you to react in a damaging way? How did you react? How did you feel as a result?

_____

_____

_____

_____

_____

_____

_____

_____

_____

_____

_____

_____

_____

_____

_____

Next, write about how you might handle the situation differently in the future, using some of the strategies you have learned.

_____

_____

_____

_____

_____

_____

_____

_____

_____

_____

_____

_____

You can use the lines in this book. You may want to download extra pages so that you can rewrite your narrative over time.

KEY TAKEAWAYS

REMEMBER: THERE'S A DIFFERENCE BETWEEN ACTION AND REACTION. When you react impulsively to situations that cause you anger or frustration, your action can be a counterproductive or even destructive move.

When teens regularly direct their anger, frustration, disgust, and blame at themselves, there's a danger that they might treat themselves poorly by engaging in risky actions. If you direct your rage at others, acting upon it will almost certainly take a toll on your relationships.

Taking a pause to calm yourself before lashing out can allow you to come up with a more reasonable way of viewing the situation. Then you can brainstorm a more creative, productive response.

CHAPTER 10

SEVENTEEN TOOLS FOR YOUR ACTION-MINDSET TOOLKIT

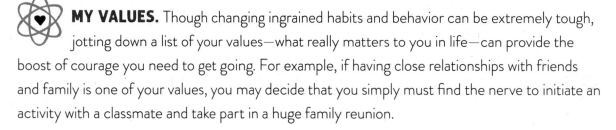

It's undeniable that the journey from avoidance to action can be scary and difficult, even when you know that making that journey is in your own best interest. But it should also be very clear by now that you have many tools at your disposal to help you muster the courage to start off and keep moving forward. Later in the chapter, you'll have an opportunity to pack your own toolkit with the ones you think will be most useful. But first, let's review what these tools are:

MY VALUES. Though changing ingrained habits and behavior can be extremely tough, jotting down a list of your values—what really matters to you in life—can provide the boost of courage you need to get going. For example, if having close relationships with friends and family is one of your values, you may decide that you simply must find the nerve to initiate an activity with a classmate and take part in a huge family reunion.

THE MOTIVATIONAL INTERVIEW. Like your list of values, this tool can help you examine your compelling reasons to act. It helps you consider how taking action will improve your quality of life. To conduct a motivational interview, ask yourself a series of questions that cause you to imagine how a given situation and your overall happiness would be affected by taking a step. If you love soccer and really would like to play, for example, imagining the fun you would be having in a week or a month if you were part of the JV team might be enough to get you to tryouts. You can review chapter 3 for a list of sample interview questions.

THE REALITY CHECK. As we've discussed, our thoughts have a major effect on our behavior, and it's frequently off-target negative self-talk that freezes teens in their tracks. You can use this tool to catch and question those thoughts. Are the thoughts accurate? Are they realistic? What is more likely true instead? What would you suggest that a friend in the same situation think?

Take a look back at activity 1 in chapter 1 to remind yourself of common off-target thinking habits that often get in the way of taking action. Do you automatically think, *I can't do that!* anytime you're faced with a new challenge? You can pause a moment, check to see if you can find any actual evidence that you can't do it, and come up with a more helpful thought instead: *I might need some practice, but I can give it a try.*

Or if you have a tendency to be a chronic worrier, to believe that anything you try will have a terrible outcome, you can quickly make a list in your head of the more likely possibilities. Developing the habit of on-target, more optimistic thinking is key to developing an action mindset.

THE SMALL STEP. Sometimes a challenge seems to require so *much* action that you throw your hands up in defeat before even trying to tackle it. You'll never be able to get your science project done by the deadline! You can't possibly manage to throw a surprise party for your friend's birthday! Try giving yourself a shot of courage by pulling out this tool. The job becomes less daunting when you break it down into a series of smaller tasks and tackle them one by one.

THE STAIRCASE EXPOSURE. This tool is sort of a variation on the small step. It's one of several, along with the next three on this list, that help you practice tolerating the feelings of acute discomfort that prevent you from taking action. One practical strategy is to plan out a staircase of less difficult incremental steps you can take on the way to your goal on the top step. This way, you expose yourself over time to a gradually growing level of discomfort, adjusting at each step and developing tolerance.

The other likely benefit of this approach: You gain confidence and hope as you succeed at taking each step. You begin to recognize that what actually happens when you act is rarely as bad as you thought it would be, and that you are able to manage just fine one step at a time.

THE IMAGINAL EXPOSURE. If even an incremental step feels too scary, you can often prepare yourself first to tolerate that discomfort by visualizing yourself taking the action before you try it. Practicing an action in your mind, walking yourself through it from start to finish, can help you get your fears to a manageable level. To revisit how to do an imaginal exposure, go to activity 22 in chapter 7.

You can find free downloads for many of these tools at http://www.newharbinger.com/50461.

BODY SENSATION (INTEROCEPTIVE) EXPOSURES. This tool is also aimed at helping you tolerate discomfort—physical discomfort. It offers relief when what you dread the most are the extremely unpleasant bodily sensations you experience when you are anxious about taking action: the racing heart, the queasy stomach, the dizziness, the dripping sweat.

The idea is to reduce the power these sensations have to keep you on the sidelines by intentionally simulating them—by spinning around in a circle, say, if concern about dizziness and queasiness is getting in your way. Or by running around the block or up a few flights of stairs to cause a racing heart and rapid breathing. The practice you get experiencing the sensations helps you discover that they are tolerable.

THE INTENTIONAL MISTAKE. Are you avoiding action because of the acute discomfort you experience at the uncertainty about whether you'll mess up? You might need to practice messing up! First you can try reminding yourself that everyone makes mistakes, and that trial and error are normal parts of making progress. If that doesn't quite do the trick, the intentional mistake exposure—purposely giving the wrong answer in class, say, or sending an email with a misspelling in it—can help you see that goofing up occasionally is usually not a big deal.

And if you often avoid social situations out of worry about looking stupid, purposely making a bad joke or some other silly move when you're with family members or a couple of close friends can have a similar effect.

MY REWARD SYSTEM. What small treats will you give yourself for each risk you take, each step that gets you closer to your goal? Planning a few ways to reward yourself—with an activity you love, a book or video game you've been wanting, even an ice cream sundae, for example—is a way to take pleasure in your efforts and encourage yourself to keep moving forward. Or maybe the problem is that you procrastinate when you feel overwhelmed, or you're unable to muster the energy to do something important because you're feeling so down. Promising yourself a small break or other treat for each period of time spent making progress can often inspire you to get going. Need ideas? Check activity 11 in chapter 4.

THE BEHAVIORAL ACTIVATION PLANNER. The idea behind behavioral activation is the interdependence principle of CBT—just as our thoughts influence our behavior, our behavior or actions also influence our thoughts. And both have a big impact on our mood.

When you're really stuck, try filling out a daily calendar for the week ahead with one or two activities per day and then just *do* them, perhaps with a friend. Chances are you'll feel more hopeful afterward.

MY SUPPORT TEAM. Can you think of trusted friends and adults or siblings whom you would feel comfortable approaching for guidance, feedback, and encouragement during times of stress or sadness? Knowing that you have people who believe in you and have your back can be an effective confidence booster when you're working up the nerve to take action. And arranging to have some company on outings in your behavioral activation planner can make the difference between following through and not.

THE READY!-SET!-GO! METER. When you're changing long-held habits, it can be helpful to track the progress you're making along the course you've set for yourself. The Ready!-Set!-Go! Meter is both a reminder of the important thinking and planning you need to do when making a change to your behavior and a way to actually visualize your courageous advance toward your goal.

SELF-COMPASSION. We often tend to be kinder and more encouraging to other people than to ourselves. Taking a moment to think about and appreciate your own great qualities and achievements can be a powerful tool. The exercise can remind you that you're capable and that it's normal and fine to make mistakes or to be shy and self-conscious in social situations. Giving yourself a dose of kindness and encouragement may also give you the confidence to try.

You can find free downloads for many of these tools at http://www.newharbinger.com/50461.

MINDFULNESS. Often, our mood and tendency to avoid taking action are rooted in spiraling anxiety or gloom about what will happen in the future and fretting or feeling down about what happened in the past. Learning to quiet the noise in your head by closing your eyes, taking deep breaths, and bringing your focus to just the present moment without judging it—tuning out everything but the sounds, the smells, the sensations of *right now*—can help you become calmer and more hopeful. For practice, you can turn to activity 16 in chapter 5.

It can also be calming to practice a more active mindfulness as you go about your daily activities. Rather than getting lost in your thoughts on a walk or bike ride, for example, you might pay close attention to the sights and sounds along the way.

PROGRESSIVE MUSCLE RELAXATION. This is a great tool to use if feelings of frustration and anger in difficult situations tend to make you react in an impulsive, harmful way rather than acting productively. That tension you frequently feel in your shoulders and neck and your clenched teeth and stomach muscles are signals that it might be helpful to calm yourself before taking an action you will later regret. This technique is often used as a good way to calm down in general.

Practicing this exercise slowly once in a while—tensing and relaxing each muscle group in your body one by one, from the top of your head to your toes—can help you gain a better sense of when your body is flashing warning signs. In that moment when you're in danger of lashing out, pausing to practice it more quickly can help you hold off and come up with a better response.

ZOOMING IN ON THE POSITIVE. This isn't a technique we've discussed before in the book, but it can be a very helpful addition to your toolkit. Spending a few minutes each evening making a list of what went well during the day—or even just okay—can be an encouraging reminder that your anxieties about what *will* happen are frequently exaggerated. A record like this can be especially useful if you have the zooming-in-on-the-negative thinking habit and often get stuck fretting obsessively about one thing that went wrong. Once you recognize a pattern—that most of what happens on most days is either not so bad or fine or even great—your perspective on life and all its possibilities is likely to become more optimistic.

GRATITUDE. Similarly, your perspective often broadens and becomes more hopeful when you practice being actively grateful, both by regularly making a list of everything and everybody you feel thankful for and by reaching out to people to say thank you. You can focus on how much you appreciate the events that happen in your life and all that you have, big and small. Feeling grateful, like focusing on what went well, can be a real mood booster! And greater optimism is apt to make you feel more capable and less likely to fear taking action.

★ ★ ★ FOR YOU TO DO ★ ★ ★

Which of the techniques that we've explored together have been—or will be—most useful to you as you cultivate your action mindset? The exercises that follow offer a way to consider all you've learned and how it can serve you.

You can find free downloads for many of these tools at http://www.newharbinger.com/50461.

Assemble Your Toolkit

Now that we've reviewed the strategies that can help you move forward, let's take a few minutes to consider which of these tools you want to pack in your personal action-mindset toolkit. Look at the list of tools below, and insert into the toolkit on the following page the ones you have found (or think you will find) to be most useful. You can do this by writing them down, by copying the icons shown here, or by drawing your own representations. Feel free to add other strategies not listed that have helped you take action. For example, if you find that a long walk in the woods calms you down as effectively as a mindfulness exercise, include that. If you know from experience that the promise of an hour with a good mystery novel is a sure way to reward yourself for pushing through your discomfort, draw a picture of a book.

Having a visual representation of your most helpful tools serves as a reminder to put them to use. In fact, you might want to take a photo of your toolkit and keep the picture handy on your phone. As you continue to make progress and add new tools, you can update the photo.

ACTION-MINDSET TOOLKIT

MY VALUES

THE MOTIVATIONAL INTERVIEW

THE REALITY CHECK

THE SMALL STEP

THE STAIRCASE EXPOSURE

THE IMAGINAL EXPOSURE

BODY SENSATION EXPOSURES

THE INTENTIONAL MISTAKE

MY REWARD SYSTEM

THE BEHAVIORAL ACTIVATION PLANNER

MY SUPPORT TEAM

THE READY!-SET!-GO! METER

SELF-COMPASSION

MINDFULNESS

PROGRESSIVE MUSCLE RELAXATION

ZOOMING IN ON THE POSITIVE

GRATITUDE

★ ★ ★ **MY ACTION-MINDSET TOOLKIT** ★ ★

Tell Your Success Story

Finally, document the story of an effort to take action or a success that you're proud of. You can write it below as if you were making an entry in your journal. Perhaps you can make a voice recording as if you were hosting a podcast. Tell the whole story, including what action you wanted to take, what was holding you back, why acting was important to you, what effort you made or what success you achieved, which tools you used to make headway, and how you felt emotionally and physically before acting and afterward.

You can reread your story anytime you feel yourself backsliding or need a boost of self-confidence. Sharing your story with someone you trust can also make you feel great.

 Download a blank journal page at http://www.newharbinger.com/50461.

_____

_____

_____

_____

_____

_____

_____

_____

_____

KEY TAKEAWAYS

WE HOPE THAT THIS BOOK HAS HELPED YOU reflect on what it is that's preventing you from fully engaging in the adventure that is your life. And we hope it helps you see—and believe—that by taking a chance on action, even when you're afraid to, you're seizing your power to shape that adventure in ways that will be most fulfilling to you. Developing a belief in your own agency—your ability to influence how your life unfolds—is key to becoming a more resilient person, able to cope with the inevitable setbacks and disappointments you'll experience. And you'll be opening yourself to the possibility of greater happiness. **GOOD LUCK ON YOUR JOURNEY!**

ACKNOWLEDGMENTS

We gratefully acknowledge the foundational work done by B. F. Skinner, Ivan Pavlov, Albert Bandura, Donald Meichenbaum, Aaron Beck, David Burns, David Barlow, Martin Seligman, and others in the development of cognitive behavioral therapy. We also acknowledge those contributions made by academic researchers and practicing therapists who have enriched the field of CBT, further expanding it to include, for example, behavioral activation (Peter Lewinsohn, Neil S. Jacobson, Sona Dimidjian, Christopher Martell, Carl W. Lejuez, and others) and mindfulness. We also acknowledge William R. Miller and Stephen Rollnick for developing motivational interviewing and Steven Hayes for his work incorporating values into therapy.

We're especially grateful to Carlo DiClemente, a pioneer with James Prochaska in expanding our understanding of the difficult process of behavior change and of the stages one goes through to succeed and maintain change. Their work informs much of the advice we share in this workbook and inspired our progress-measuring tool, the Ready!-Set!-Go! Meter. We greatly appreciate Dr. DiClemente's willingness to review our manuscript and to write the foreword.

I, Mary Alvord, wish to offer my sincere appreciation to all the teens who have worked with me over the years. I have been honored with their willingness to delve into distressing thoughts, feelings, and actions and with their continuing efforts to better their lives.

We thank all the clinicians from Alvord, Baker & Associates who have provided support and feedback as we developed this book: Drs. Candice Watson, Anahi Collado, Keri Linas, Heather Loffredo, Colleen Cummings, Nina Shiffrin, Kelly O'Brien, Lem Yutzy, Elizabeth Malesa, Sue Wilson, Andrea Chisholm, Erin Lewis-Morrarty, Lynn Bufka, Rebecca Abrahams, Betsy Carmichael, and Tom Verratti. We want to acknowledge the New Harbinger team, with particular gratitude to Tesilya Hanauer for her professionalism, advocacy, and guidance. Finally, special thanks to Marie Picini and John McManus for reviewing the manuscript.

RESOURCES

ORGANIZATIONS

American Psychological Association (APA) https://www.apa.org
The APA's topics page can be searched for general information, tip sheets, and resources on a variety of mental health and mind-body issues.

American Psychological Association (APA) Annual Stress in America Survey
https://www.apa.org/news/press/releases/stress.pdf
The APA has been conducting annual surveys since 2007 measuring stress across the country. The surveys report the leading sources of stress, common behaviors used to manage stress, and the impact of stress on the lives of adults, children, and teens. The connections between mind and body are highlighted.

Anxiety and Depression Association of America (ADAA) https://adaa.org
ADAA is an international nonprofit organization dedicated to the prevention, treatment, and cure of anxiety, depression, OCD, PTSD, and co-occurring disorders through the alignment of science, treatment, and education. Explore ADAA's Understand Anxiety and Depression page to learn more about the causes of anxiety disorders and depression, as well as ADAA's Find Help page for treatment and support resources, tips, and tools for parents and teens and more.

Association for Behavioral and Cognitive Therapies (ABCT) https://www.abct.org
ABCT is an organization committed to investigating and applying evidence-based behavioral, cognitive, and other approaches to treating psychological problems. Three particular sections are of interest to teens: "Get Help," "Get Information," and "Fact Sheets."

Centers for Disease Control and Prevention (CDC) http://www.cdc.gov
This CDC webpage provides a list of publications and other resources focused on adolescent health and mental health.

The Centre for Clinical Interventions (CCI) http://www.healthywa.wa.gov.au/Articles/A_E/Anxiety-and-panic
Based in Australia, the CCI posts various treatment modules on anxiety, behavioral activation, perfectionism, and self-compassion. Explore the site for others on topics of your interest.

Substance Abuse and Mental Health Services Administration (SAMHSA) https://www.samhsa.gov
Part of the U.S. Department of Health and Human Services, SAMHSA provides numerous resources and, under the "Find Help & Treatment" tab, notes the new 988 hotline number to the National Suicide Prevention Lifeline and other sources of help, including a Behavioral Health Treatment Services Locator.

APPS

Consider using your smartphone or other device to set reminders to notice your thoughts and mood, develop some coping actions, and practice some mindfulness exercises.

You might also consider downloading free apps such as Breathe2Relax, Mindfulness Coach, and Virtual Hope Box.

Though originally designed by the National Center for Telehealth & Technology and the Department of Defense for military personnel and their families, these free apps are available to the general public for Apple and Android devices. They are useful tools for teens to use as a supplement to treatment. The apps provide relaxation audios, mood monitoring, and behavioral activation plans and strategies to develop positive self-talk and improve mood.

CDS AND DIGITAL DOWNLOADS

Relaxation and Self-Regulation Techniques for Children and Teens: Mastering the Mind-Body Connection offers teens a variety of strategies that can support their efforts to change thought habits. The recordings help increase awareness of one's thoughts and physiological reactions to situations. Listeners have the opportunity to practice skills within each track. Recordings include self-talk and mindfulness, as well as recordings to calm and regulate the mind and body through visualization, progressive muscle relaxation, and calm and attentive breathing. The majority of the scripts are based on cognitive behavioral therapy (CBT) and borrow from Eastern traditions of meditation (Alvord, Zucker, and Alvord 2011).

Relaxation and Wellness Techniques: Mastering the Mind-Body Connection is a helpful resource to support the efforts of noticing and making changes to thinking habits. Targeted toward older teens and adults, this CD provides ten recordings with CBT techniques and meditative tracks to help achieve a sense of calm and a quieter mind. For example, a recording titled "Challenging Your Catastrophic Thoughts" specifically addresses anxious "what if" thinking and leads the listener through the process of questioning their unhelpful thoughts. Visualization, progressive muscle relaxation, breathing approaches, mindfulness, and Eastern meditation practices round out the CD, which is also available as individual digital downloads from Amazon and iTunes (Alvord, Zucker, and Alvord 2013).

FURTHER READING

Alvord, M. K., and A. McGrath. 2017. *Conquer Negative Thinking for Teens: A Workbook to Break the Nine Thought Habits That Are Holding You Back.* Oakland, CA: New Harbinger Publications.

Galanti, R. 2020. *Anxiety Relief for Teens: Essential CBT Skills and Self-Care Practices to Overcome Anxiety and Stress.* New York: Zeitgeist Young Adult.

Schab, L. 2022. *The Self-Esteem Workbook for Teens: Activities to Help You Build Confidence and Achieve Your Goals.* Oakland, CA: New Harbinger Publications.

Seligman, M. E. 2011. *Flourish.* New York: Free Press.

Shannon, J. 2022. *The Shyness and Social Anxiety Workbook for Teens.* Oakland, CA: New Harbinger Publications.

Zucker, B. 2022. *A Perfectionist's Guide to Not Being Perfect.* Washington, DC: Magination Press.

REFERENCES

Alvord, M. K., and A. McGrath. 2017. *Conquer Negative Thinking for Teens: A Workbook to Break the Nine Thought Habits That Are Holding You Back.* Oakland, CA: New Harbinger Publications.

Anderson, K. 2019. *Who Is Michael Jordan?* New York: Penguin Workshop.

Hayes, S., and S. Smith. 2005. *Get Out of Your Mind and Into Your Life: The New Acceptance and Commitment Therapy.* Oakland, CA: New Harbinger Publications.

Jobs, S. 2005. Stanford University graduation speech, Stanford, California, June 12. https://news.stanford.edu/2005/06/14/jobs-061505.

Leahy, R. L. 2005. *The Worry Cure: Seven Steps to Stop Worry from Stopping You.* New York: Three Rivers Press.

Miller, W. R., and S. Rollnick. 2012. *Motivational Interviewing: Helping People Change.* 3rd ed. New York: Guilford Press.

The Nobel Prize. n.d. "Sir Alexander Fleming." https://www.nobelprize.org/prizes/medicine/1945/fleming/facts.

Prochaska, J. O., and C. C. DiClemente. 1982. "Transtheoretical Therapy: Toward a More Integrative Model of Change." *Psychotherapy: Theory, Research and Practice,* 19, 76–288. http://dx.doi.org/10.1037/h0088437

Seligman, M. E. 1995. *The Optimistic Child.* Boston: Houghton Mifflin Company.

Did you know there are **free tools** you can download for this book?

Free tools are things like **worksheets**, **guided meditation exercises**, and **more** that will help you get the most out of your book.

You can download free tools for this book— whether you bought or borrowed it, in any format, from any source—from the New Harbinger website. All you need is a NewHarbinger.com account. Just use the URL provided in this book to view the free tools that are available for it. Then, click on the "download" button for the free tool you want, and follow the prompts that appear to log in to your NewHarbinger.com account and download the material.

You can also save the free tools for this book to your **Free Tools Library** so you can access them again anytime, just by logging in to your account! Just look for this button on the book's free tools page.

+ Save this to my free tools library

If you need help accessing or downloading free tools, visit **newharbinger.com/faq** or contact us at **customerservice@newharbinger.com.**

MARY KARAPETIAN ALVORD, PHD, is a psychologist with more than forty years of clinical experience; and is director of Alvord, Baker & Associates. She specializes in treating children, adolescents, and adults using evidence-based therapies. She is adjunct associate professor of psychiatry and behavioral sciences at The George Washington University School of Medicine and Health Sciences. Fellow of both the American Psychological Association (APA) and the Association for Behavioral and Cognitive Therapies (ABCT), she is also a clinical fellow of the Anxiety and Depression Association of America (ADAA). Recently, she founded a nonprofit—Resilience Across Borders, Inc.—with a mission to promote mental health. She is coauthor of *Resilience Builder Program for Children and Adolescents*, and with Anne McGrath, *Conquer Negative Thinking for Teens*.

ANNE MCGRATH, MA, is an editor and writer with expertise in health, medicine, mental health, and education. She retired as executive editor overseeing publications and events at *U.S. News & World Report*, where she was responsible for the annual Best Hospitals and Best Colleges annual special issues—and spent thirty-five years writing and editing on health, medicine, higher education, and personal finance. She is coauthor of *Conquer Negative Thinking for Teens*. She holds a master's in journalism from Syracuse University.

Foreword writer **CARLO DICLEMENTE, PHD,** is Professor Emeritus of Psychology at the University of Maryland, Baltimore County (UMBC). He is codeveloper of the transtheoretical model of behavior change, and author of *Changing for Good* and *Addiction and Change*, as well as several professional books.

More  Instant Help Books for Teens

An Imprint of New Harbinger Publications

THE SELF-CONFIDENCE WORKBOOK FOR TEENS

Mindfulness Skills to Help You Overcome Social Anxiety, Be Assertive, and Believe in Yourself

978-1648480492 / US $18.95

PUT YOUR WORRIES HERE

A Creative Journal for Teens with Anxiety

978-1684032143 / US $18.95

THE GIRL'S GUIDE TO RELATIONSHIPS, SEXUALITY, AND CONSENT

Tools to Help Teens Stay Safe, Empowered, and Confident

978-1684039739 / US $17.95

JUST AS YOU ARE

A Teen's Guide to Self-Acceptance and Lasting Self-Esteem

978-1626255906 / US $17.95

OVERCOMING SUICIDAL THOUGHTS FOR TEENS

CBT Activities to Reduce Pain, Increase Hope, and Build Meaningful Connections

978-1684039975 / US $18.95

THE RESILIENT TEEN

10 Key Skills to Bounce Back from Setbacks and Turn Stress into Success

978-1684035786 / US $17.95

newharbinger**publications**

1-800-748-6273 / newharbinger.com

(VISA, MC, AMEX / prices subject to change without notice)

Follow Us 🔲 📘 🐦 ▶️ 📌 💼

Don't miss out on new books from New Harbinger.
Subscribe to our email list at **newharbinger.com/subscribe**